Android for the BeagleBone Black

Design and implement Android apps that interface with your own custom hardware circuits and the BeagleBone Black

Andrew Henderson

Aravind Prakash

[PACKT] PUBLISHING

BIRMINGHAM - MUMBAI

Android for the BeagleBone Black

First published: February 2015

Production reference: 1130215

Published by Packt Publishing Ltd.
Livery Place
35 Livery Street
Birmingham B3 2PB, UK.

ISBN 978-1-78439-216-1

www.packtpub.com

Credits

Authors
Andrew Henderson

Aravind Prakash

Reviewers
Nathan Burles

Guy Carpenter

Anuj Deshpande

Commissioning Editor
Amarabha Banerjee

Acquisition Editor
Greg Wild

Content Development Editor
Neetu Ann Mathew

Technical Editor
Tanvi Bhatt

Copy Editors
Deepa Nambiar

Vikrant Phadke

Project Coordinator
Mary Alex

Proofreaders
Simran Bhogal

Bernadette Watkins

Indexer
Hemangini Bari

Graphics
Sheetal Aute

Production Coordinator
Manu Joseph

Cover Work
Manu Joseph

About the Authors

Andrew Henderson has over 15 years of experience developing software for the Linux desktop and embedded Linux and Android systems. He is currently a PhD candidate at Syracuse University, with research interests in the areas of system security and dynamic analysis. He maintains multiple open source projects for the BeagleBoard and BeagleBone platforms.

I want to thank Cheryl, Olivia, and my father for all of their encouragement and support during the time that I spent researching and writing the material for this book. I would also like to thank Dr. Heng Yin, Dr. Wenliang Du, and Dr. Ehat Ercanli of Syracuse University for lending their knowledge and guidance to my Android OS and BeagleBone/BeagleBoard research.

Aravind Prakash is a PhD candidate at Syracuse University. His interests lie in system and mobile security, with emphasis on program analysis. He has published in multiple top-tier computer-security conferences. He brings with him over a decade of programming experience from companies such as Microsoft, McAfee, and FireEye.

About the Reviewers

Nathan Burles is a post-doctoral researcher with a PhD in computer science. He is currently working for the University of York, on subjects as diverse as artificial neural networks and dynamic, adaptive, and automated software engineering.

In his free time, he enjoys tinkering with embedded systems and electronics, ranging from full systems such as the Raspberry Pi and BeagleBone Black to simple microcontrollers such as the Arduino—adding circuitry to communicate using 433MHz RF and infrared.

Nathan blogs about his projects as well as topics including website development, Android, and dancing at http://www.nburles.co.uk.

Guy Carpenter is a software developer and veteran hacker. He has contributed code to the BeagleBone, Raspberry Pi, Arduino, and Chumby Hackers Board communities. He owns Clearwater Software in Brisbane, Australia.

Anuj Deshpande adores the Beaglebone Black and all things embedded with Linux. He is an active part of the local hackerspace, Doo, in Pune, and regularly hosts meet-ups on a variety of topics.

Some of the projects that he has been a part of are Userspace Arduino, PixHawk Fire, and Tah. He was an intern at Beagleboard.org, Oneirix Labs, as well as 3D Robotics for a brief period of time. Anuj completed his bachelor's degree in computer science from PICT, Pune.

www.PacktPub.com

Support files, eBooks, discount offers, and more

For support files and downloads related to your book, please visit www.PacktPub.com.

Did you know that Packt offers eBook versions of every book published, with PDF and ePub files available? You can upgrade to the eBook version at www.PacktPub.com and as a print book customer, you are entitled to a discount on the eBook copy. Get in touch with us at service@packtpub.com for more details.

At www.PacktPub.com, you can also read a collection of free technical articles, sign up for a range of free newsletters and receive exclusive discounts and offers on Packt books and eBooks.

https://www2.packtpub.com/books/subscription/packtlib

Do you need instant solutions to your IT questions? PacktLib is Packt's online digital book library. Here, you can search, access, and read Packt's entire library of books.

Why subscribe?

- Fully searchable across every book published by Packt
- Copy and paste, print, and bookmark content
- On demand and accessible via a web browser

Free access for Packt account holders

If you have an account with Packt at www.PacktPub.com, you can use this to access PacktLib today and view 9 entirely free books. Simply use your login credentials for immediate access.

Table of Contents

Preface

The broad availability of Android-based devices has generated a large amount of interest in developing software applications, or apps, that target Android. Luckily, a powerful and low-cost hardware platform is available that allows you to quickly and easily test your apps on real hardware: the BeagleBone Black. With a focus on small size and a wide variety of expansion and interfacing opportunities, the BeagleBone Black provides a lot of processing power at a very low price. It also provides an opportunity to app developers that once belonged only to those that were expert hardware hackers or owners of expensive hardware development kits: the chance to write Android apps that interact with custom hardware circuits.

Whether you are brand new to hardware interfacing or a seasoned expert, *Android for the BeagleBone Black* provides you with the tools that you need to begin creating Android apps that communicate directly with your custom hardware. From the very beginning, this book will help you understand Android's unique approach to hardware interfacing. You will install and customize Android, build circuits that interface with your BeagleBone Black platform, and build native code and Android apps that use that hardware to communicate with the outside world. By sequentially working through the examples in each chapter, you will learn how to create multithreaded apps that are capable of interfacing with multiple hardware components simultaneously.

Once you have explored the variety of example circuits and apps in this book, you will be well on your way toward becoming an Android hardware interfacing pro!

What this book covers

Chapter 1, *Introduction to Android and the BeagleBone Black*, walks you through the process of installing the Android OS to your BeagleBone Black board. It also provides you with a list of hardware components that you will need to perform the activities throughout this book.

Chapter 2, *Interfacing with Android*, introduces you to several aspects of the BeagleBone Black's hardware and Android's Hardware Abstraction Layer. It describes how to make a few modifications to both your development environment and Android installed on your BeagleBone Black to allow Android apps to access the various hardware features of the BeagleBone Black.

Chapter 3, *Handling Inputs and Outputs with GPIOs*, guides you through building your very first hardware interfacing circuit and explains the details of a basic Android app that can communicate with it. This is your first step toward building much more complex apps that interact with the world outside your BeagleBone Black.

Chapter 4, *Storing and Retrieving Data with I2C*, expands on the basics from *Chapter 3*, *Handling Inputs and Outputs with GPIOs*, and explains how asynchronous background threads within your apps are used to communicate with hardware. It guides you through building a circuit that interfaces a nonvolatile memory chip to the BeagleBone Black and the implementation details of an app that interacts with the chip.

Chapter 5, *Interfacing with High-speed Sensors Using SPI*, explores creating apps that perform high-speed interfacing using a temperature and pressure sensor interfaced to the BeagleBone Black.

Chapter 6, *Creating a Complete Interfacing Solution*, combines the lessons learned about GPIO, I2C, and SPI interfacing from the previous chapters to create a single, complex hardware and software solution that uses all three interfaces to react to hardware events that originate from the outside world.

Chapter 7, *Where to Go from Here*, describes a few more of the hardware interfaces available on the BeagleBone Black, explains how to create more permanent Android hardware/software solutions, and gives you a few ideas for future projects to explore.

What you need for this book

We have provided instructions in this book assuming that you are using either a Windows- or Linux-based computer. If you are already an Android app developer, you probably have all of the software applications that you need already installed. We expect you to have both the Eclipse ADT and Android NDK already installed, though we provide links to download these tools at the start of *Chapter 2, Interfacing with Android*, in the event that you do not already have them. *Chapter 1, Introduction to Android and the BeagleBone Black*, provides a list of the various hardware components and equipment that you will need to implement the example interfacing circuits used throughout the book.

Who this book is for

If you are an Android app developer who wants to begin experimenting with the hardware capabilities of the BeagleBone Black platform, then this book is ideal for you. Having familiarity with basic electronics principles is helpful, and the reader is expected to have basic knowledge in developing Android apps with the Eclipse ADT and Android SDK, but no prior hardware experience is required.

Conventions

In this book, you will find a number of text styles that distinguish between different kinds of information. Here are some examples of these styles and an explanation of their meaning.

Code words in text, database table names, folder names, filenames, file extensions, pathnames, dummy URLs, user input, and Twitter handles are shown as follows: "This avoids having to include a special module and an overlay that loads commands in your init.{ro.hardware}.rc file."

A block of code is set as follows:

```
extern int openFRAM(const unsigned int bus, const unsigned int
address);
extern int readFRAM(const unsigned int offset, const unsigned int
    bufferSize, const char *buffer);
extern int writeFRAM(const unsigned int offset, const unsigned int
    const char *buffer);
extern void closeFRAM(void);
```

When we wish to draw your attention to a particular part of a code block, the relevant lines or items are set in bold:

```
public void onClickSaveButton(View view) {
   hwTask = new HardwareTask();
   hwTask.saveToFRAM(this);
}

public void onClickLoadButton(View view) {
   hwTask = new HardwareTask();
   hwTask.loadFromFRAM(this);
}
```

Any command-line input or output is written as follows:

```
root@beagleboneblack:/ # i2cdetect -y -r 2
```

New terms and **important words** are shown in bold. Words that you see on the screen, for example, in menus or dialog boxes, appear in the text like this: "If the user clicks on the **Sample** button once more, another HardwareTask instance is instantiated."

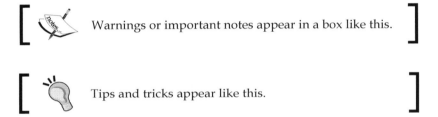

Warnings or important notes appear in a box like this.

Tips and tricks appear like this.

Reader feedback

Feedback from our readers is always welcome. Let us know what you think about this book—what you liked or disliked. Reader feedback is important for us as it helps us develop titles that you will really get the most out of.

To send us general feedback, simply e-mail feedback@packtpub.com, and mention the book's title in the subject of your message.

If there is a topic that you have expertise in and you are interested in either writing or contributing to a book, see our author guide at www.packtpub.com/authors.

Customer support

Now that you are the proud owner of a Packt book, we have a number of things to help you to get the most from your purchase.

Downloading the example code

You can download the example code files from your account at http://www. packtpub.com for all the Packt Publishing books you have purchased. If you purchased this book elsewhere, you can visit http://www.packtpub.com/support and register to have the files e-mailed directly to you.

Errata

Although we have taken every care to ensure the accuracy of our content, mistakes do happen. If you find a mistake in one of our books—maybe a mistake in the text or the code—we would be grateful if you could report this to us. By doing so, you can save other readers from frustration and help us improve subsequent versions of this book. If you find any errata, please report them by visiting http://www.packtpub. com/submit-errata, selecting your book, clicking on the **Errata Submission Form** link, and entering the details of your errata. Once your errata are verified, your submission will be accepted and the errata will be uploaded to our website or added to any list of existing errata under the Errata section of that title.

To view the previously submitted errata, go to https://www.packtpub.com/books/content/support and enter the name of the book in the search field. The required information will appear under the **Errata** section.

Piracy

Piracy of copyrighted material on the Internet is an ongoing problem across all media. At Packt, we take the protection of our copyright and licenses very seriously. If you come across any illegal copies of our works in any form on the Internet, please provide us with the location address or website name immediately so that we can pursue a remedy.

Please contact us at copyright@packtpub.com with a link to the suspected pirated material.

We appreciate your help in protecting our authors and our ability to bring you valuable content.

Questions

If you have a problem with any aspect of this book, you can contact us at questions@packtpub.com, and we will do our best to address the problem.

1

Introduction to Android and the BeagleBone Black

In this book, you'll learn how to install Android to a microSD card for use with the BeagleBone Black and create Android apps that interface with external hardware that is connected to the BeagleBone Black. You will develop software that receives input from the outside world via buttons and sensors, stores and retrieves data from external memory chips, and lights external LEDs. Better yet, you'll learn how to do this in a flexible way that can be easily integrated into your apps.

As you explore the world of interfacing hardware with Android, you will discover that it encompasses many different areas of expertise. Understanding electronic circuits and knowing how to interface them with the BeagleBone Black, understanding the Linux kernel, and developing Android apps are a few such areas. Luckily, you don't have to be an expert in these areas to learn the basics of interfacing hardware with Android. We have done our best to guide you through the examples in this book without requiring you to have an in-depth knowledge of the Linux kernel or electronics theory.

In this chapter, we will cover the following topics:

- Looking back on Android and BeagleBone Black development
- Shopping for the hardware essentials
- Learning about the hardware you'll interface with
- Installing Android on the BeagleBone Black

Looking back on Android and BeagleBone Black development

The Android operating system has been taking the world by storm. Ever since its introduction to the world in a beta release in 2007, it has grown to become the dominant mobile phone OS. Aside from mobile phones, it has also been used for tablets (such as the Barnes & Noble Nook eReader and the Tesco Hudl tablet) and a variety of other embedded multimedia devices. The OS has added new features and evolved over the years, but it still has the same primary design principles as it did when it was first conceived. It provides a lightweight OS with a touchscreen interface that gives quick and easy access to multimedia applications while using minimal resources.

Aside from its general popularity, Android has a number of advantages that make it an excellent OS for your projects. The source code of Android is open source and freely available from http://source.android.com. It is free for you to use in any products that you create. Android uses the popular Linux kernel, so any expertise that you already have with Linux will aid you in your Android development. There is a well-documented interfacing API that makes developing for Android simple and straightforward.

The broad availability of Android-based devices has generated a large amount of interest in developing software applications, or apps, that target Android. It has become easier to develop Android apps. Eclipse **Android Development Tools (ADT)** allows app developers to prototype software and then execute that software within an emulated Android device environment. However, the emulated device differs from real hardware in subtle (and sometimes dramatic) ways in terms of speed and appearance. Luckily, a powerful and low-cost hardware platform is available that allows you to quickly and easily test your apps on real hardware: the BeagleBone Black.

The **BeagleBone Black (BBB)** hardware platform, produced by **CircuitCo** for the BeagleBoard.org nonprofit organization, is a newcomer to the open source hardware scene. First produced in 2013, this low-cost, ARM-based single board computer is an improvement over the original BeagleBone platform. The BBB is an improvement over the original BeagleBone board that offers increased processing power, built-in HDMI video, and either a 2 or 4 GB (depending upon the BBB's revision) on-board eMMC memory. With a focus on small size and a wide variety of expansion and interfacing opportunities, the BBB provides a lot of processing power at a very low price. The following image shows a typical BBB:

The BeagleBone Black (Source: www.beagleboard.org)

Android runs on the inexpensive BBB, which makes it an excellent hardware platform to use to explore Android and develop your own custom Android projects, for example, if you had an idea for an Android kiosk device, a hand-held gaming console, or some other multimedia device. The combination of Android and the BBB will allow you to prototype such devices quickly and cheaply.

Now that we have taken a quick look at the BBB and Android, let's take a look at the hardware that you will need to make the most out of both of them.

Shopping for the hardware essentials

When you purchase your BBB, you will only receive the board and a USB cable to power and communicate with it. Before you begin any serious software development for hardware-interfacing projects with the BBB, there are a few additional pieces of hardware that you will need. In our opinion, the best place to purchase these items is **AdaFruit** (www.adafruit.com). Almost everything here is available from this single source, and their customer service is very good. In fact, many of the items listed here are available as a BeagleBone Black starter kit from AdaFruit (product ID 703). The starter kit does not contain a 3.3 V **Future Technology Devices International (FTDI)** cable, but it does include the BeagleBone Black itself.

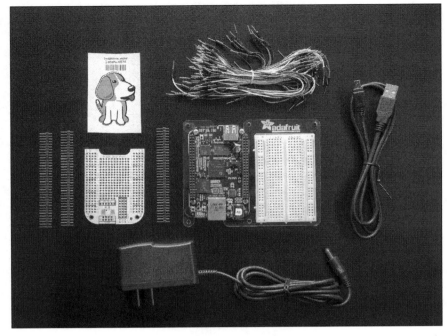

Contents of the BeagleBone Black starter kit from AdaFruit (source: www.adafruit.com)

The FTDI cable

A 3.3 volt FTDI cable (product ID 70) allows you to view all of the serial debug output of the BBB. If you are performing any serious development, you must have one of these cables. The cable is necessary if you wish to observe the boot process of the BBB (both bootloader and kernel output as the system is initialized), and it also provides a console shell into Linux and Android. This shell helps you to troubleshoot boot problems, as you will always have a method of interacting with the system when a network connection is unavailable, or when no communication services are up and running.

Power supply

While the BBB can be powered via the USB cable, this method supplies barely enough power to run the BBB. If you are using external capes, or are otherwise attaching external circuits that draw power from the 5 volt pins of the BBB, you must use an external power supply. BeagleBoard.org specifies that the power supply must be a 2 amp, 5 volt DC power supply with a 2.1 mm barrel connector that is center positive. AdaFruit sells a power supply that conforms to the BBB's requirements (product ID 276).

Breadboard and the mounting plate

Experimenting with electronics becomes much simpler if you are able to easily and quickly construct circuits without the worry of soldering. Because of this, we recommend that you invest in a breadboard and some breadboarding jumper wires (product ID 153). Your breadboard doesn't have to be anything big or fancy, but you should use at least a standard half-size breadboard (product ID 64) for the projects given in this book.

AdaFruit Proto Plate (product ID 702) is an additional item that we recommend that you purchase. Proto Plate is a plastic plate that both the BBB and a half-size breadboard mount onto. This helps you avoid accidentally stretching or disconnecting the wires that connect electronic circuits to the BBB. Using Proto Plate makes relocating your BBB and breadboard simple and painless.

MicroSD cards

If you do much work with the BBB, you'll always want to have a few extra microSD cards around! Android will fit onto an 8 GB microSD card with plenty of free space available to hold your own apps. You can write an Android image to a larger microSD card, but most premade Android system images will only consume the first 4–8 GB of space on the card. As most laptops and desktop PCs don't directly accept microSD cards, you should own at least one microSD-to-SD card adapter. Luckily, one of these adapters is typically packaged with each microSD card that you buy.

Learning about the hardware you'll interface with

The best way to learn about interfacing Android software with hardware is to learn while having real hardware components connected to your BBB. This way, your software will talk to actual hardware and you can directly observe how your apps respond to physical interaction with your system. We have selected a variety of electronic components that will be used throughout the book to demonstrate various aspects of hardware interfacing. You are welcome to use as many or as few of these components as your interests and budget permit. It can be expensive to purchase all of these components at once, but make sure to buy all of the components necessary for each chapter if you are interested in implementing the examples in that chapter.

General-purpose components

In *Chapter 3, Handling Inputs and Outputs with GPIOs*, and *Chapter 6, Creating a Complete Interfacing Solution*, you will use a variety of electronic components such as pushbuttons, LEDs, and resistors to interface with the BBB. Many of these items can be purchased from any electronics supplier, such as **DigiKey** (www.digikey.com), **Mouser Electronics** (www.mouser.com), and **SparkFun** (www.sparkfun.com). Both Digikey and Mouser offer so many variants of each available component that it can be difficult for an inexperienced hardware hacker to pick the right components to buy. Because of this, we will recommend a few products from SparkFun that will give you suitable components needed to complete the exercises in this book. You are welcome to select your components from another supplier if using a different one is more convenient for you.

Our examples require only three components: a resistor, a pushbutton switch, and an LED. We suggest purchasing a 1K ohm, 1/6 (or 1/4) watt resistor (part #COM-08980), a 12 mm push button switch (part #COM-09190), and any small LED (3–10 mm in size) that can be triggered by around 3 volt or less (part #COM-12903 is a good assortment of 5 mm LEDs).

The AdaFruit memory breakout board

In *Chapter 4, Storing and Retrieving Data with I2C*, and *Chapter 6, Creating a Complete Interfacing Solution*, you will interface with a 32 KB **Ferroelectric Random Access Memory (FRAM)**, which is a nonvolatile memory IC, to store and retrieve data. We have selected AdaFruit Breakout Board (product ID 1895) that contains this IC. The breakout board already contains all of the necessary components to interface the IC to the BBB, so you need not worry about many of the low-level details involved in creating a clean, noise-free connection between each IC and the BBB.

The FRAM Breakout Board with its header strip (source: www.adafruit.com)

The AdaFruit sensor breakout board

In *Chapter 5*, *Interfacing with High-speed Sensors Using SPI*, and *Chapter 6*, *Creating a Complete Interfacing Solution*, you will interface with a sensor IC to receive environmental data. We have selected an AdaFruit breakout board (product ID 1900) that contains these ICs. These breakout boards already contain all of the necessary components to interface the ICs to the BBB, so you need not worry about many of the low-level details involved in creating a clean, noise-free connection between each IC and the BBB.

Preparing the breakout boards

Each breakout board comes with a header strip. This header strip must be soldered into each breakout board so that they can be easily connected to the breadboard. This is the only soldering that is required to complete the exercises in this book. If you are unfamiliar with soldering, there are numerous tutorials online that explain techniques for effective soldering. If you feel uncomfortable soldering the header strips, ask a friend, instructor, or colleague to assist you with the process.

A few online soldering tutorials that we suggest that you check out are:

- https://www.youtube.com/watch?v=BLfXXRfRIzY
- https://learn.sparkfun.com/tutorials/how-to-solder---through-hole-soldering

Installing Android on the BeagleBone Black

The Android OS is a complex piece of software that is constructed out of many components built from a very large codebase. It can be a difficult and time-consuming task to build Android from source, so you will be using a premade Android image from the **BBBAndroid** project (www.bbbandroid.org) throughout this book.

BBBAndroid is a port of **Android Open Source Project** (**AOSP**) KitKat Android to the BBB. There are a few different distributions of Android available for the BBB, but we selected BBBAndroid because it uses the 3.8 Linux kernel. This kernel includes the **Cape Manager** (**capemgr**) functionality as well as a few other tools that will assist you in interfacing hardware to Android apps. Other flavors of Android on the BBB use the 3.2 Linux kernel, which is much older and lacks capemgr support. *Chapter 2*, *Interfacing with Android*, discusses the capemgr functionality in more detail. The 3.8 kernel is a good balance between enabling the newer features for the BBB while avoiding any potentially unstable, cutting-edge features.

The BBB can boot its OS in a few different ways:

- **Onboard eMMC**: The OS resides within the onboard eMMC storage. The Angstrom or Debian OS that comes installed on your BBB boots from the eMMC out of the box.

- **MicroSD card**: The OS resides on a microSD card that is inserted into the BBB. If a bootloader is installed on the microSD card, the bootloader installed on the onboard eMMC notices the presence of the microSD and will boot from that instead. In addition, booting from the microSD card is forced when the **user boot** button is held down during BBB power up.

- **Over the network**: The bootloader is capable of downloading a kernel over the network via TFTP. The OS can actually be downloaded at boot time though this is usually only done during commercial product development. This is an advanced feature that is outside the scope of this book.

The BBBAndroid image is designed to be written to and booted from a microSD card. As the image creates a fully bootable system on the microSD card, you will not have to hold the BBB's **user boot** button during power on to boot into Android. Simply insert the microSD card into the BBB and you'll boot into Android automatically.

Using a microSD card-based OS is advantageous for us because you can easily mount the card on a Linux PC to modify the Android filesystem as you see fit. If the OS is installed in the eMMC, it can be hard to access the OS to change arbitrary files in the filesystem. The system must be running to access the eMMC contents, so making a change that corrupts the system or makes it unbootable makes accessing the eMMC to fix the problem difficult.

Downloading a premade Android image

The main page of the BBBAndroid website provides a download link for the most recent premade image. Like any open source project, details about the version number and size of each image are likely to change over time as bugs are found and changes are made. However, the latest and greatest will be available via the website.

BBBAndroid's images are compressed using the xz compressor utility to save time when downloading, so the image must be decompressed prior to writing it to a microSD card. The tools used to decompress and write the image will vary depending upon the OS that you are using. While the compressed image might only be a few hundred MB in size, the uncompressed image will be 8 GB.

Prior to beginning the decompression of the image, make sure that you have enough hard drive space to hold the uncompressed image.

Creating your Android microSD card using Windows

Under Windows-based OSes, the compressed image can be uncompressed using tools such as 7-Zip or WinRAR and then written to the microSD card using the tool Win32 Disk Imager. All of these tools are freely available for download. To prepare an Android microSD card, follow these steps:

1. For this example, you'll use the WinRAR application. Download WinRAR from www.rarlab.com and install it. WinRAR will integrate with the Windows Explorer shell of the Windows desktop.

2. Download and install the Win32 Disk Imager application. It is available from the project's SourceForge page at http://sourceforge.net/projects/win32diskimager.

3. Right-click on the BBBAndroid image that you downloaded and select the **Extract here** option on the Explorer shell context menu. An uncompressed version of the image (8 GB in size) will be written to the same location as the compressed image. The decompression process might take several minutes.

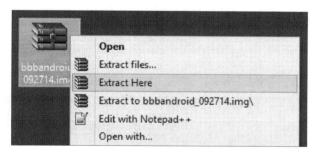

Decompress the xz-compressed image with WinRAR

4. Insert an 8+ GB microSD card into the system. The card will be detected by Windows as having a valid filesystem on it if it came preformatted (most cards are sold preformatted for your convenience). Irrespective of whether the card is formatted or not, a drive letter is assigned to it by Windows.

5. Browse to **This PC** and examine the devices shown under **Devices and drives**. The card should be shown. Make a note of the drive letter assigned to the card.

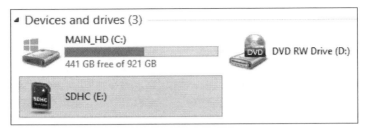

The microSD card will be shown with a drive letter under Windows (drive E in the image)

6. Launch Win32 Disk Imager. Enter the filename and path to the uncompressed image in the text field, or click on the folder icon to navigate to the file's location. Change the **Device** drop-down box to the drive letter of the microSD card that you identified in step 4.

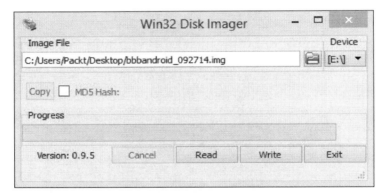

Win32 Disk Imager with the image file specified (note that the drive letter matches that of the microSD card)

7. Writing the image will take several minutes. Once the write has completed, remove the microSD card from your computer and insert it into your BBB.

8. Power on the BBB and Android will begin to boot. On the first boot, it will take several minutes for the top-level UI screen to appear. On subsequent boots, it will take only 30 to 60 seconds to reach the top-level UI screen.

Congratulations! Your BBB is now running the Android OS.

Creating your Android microSD card using Linux

Under Linux, the compressed Android image can be uncompressed using the `xz` command and written to the microSD card using the `dd` command. To prepare an Android microSD card, follow these steps:

1. Make sure that you have `xz` installed. For systems using `apt-get`, try installing the xz-utils package:

   ```
   $ sudo apt-get install xz-utils
   ```

2. Decompress the image using `xz`. Substitute the name of your image file (with the `.xz` file extension), as shown in the following command:

   ```
   $ xz --decompress [IMAGE FILENAME]
   ```

3. Once uncompressed, the image will lose its `.xz` file extension and have a size of 8 GB. Insert your microSD card into the computer. A device in the `/dev` directory will be assigned to your card. To determine which device it is, use `fdisk`:

   ```
   $ sudo fdisk -l
   ```

4. The `fdisk` utility will display all storage devices currently connected to your computer. One of the devices will report as being the same size as the microSD card. For example, if you insert an 8 GB microSD card, you will see something similar to this:

   ```
   Disk /dev/sdb: 8018 MB, 8018460672 bytes
   ```

   The exact storage capacity of the card varies slightly between manufacturers, but the size is approximately 8 GB. The device assigned to this card is `/dev/sdb`. Other devices listed by `fdisk` will be secondary storage devices (such as your hard drive). Before proceeding any further, make certain that you have identified the proper device file that belongs to your microSD card. If you select the wrong device, you will destroy the filesystem on that device!

5. Write the image to the microSD card using `dd`. Assuming that the device you identified in step 5 is `/dev/sdb`, use the following command to perform the write:

   ```
   $ sudo dd if=[NAME OF IMAGE] of=/dev/sdb bs=4M
   ```

6. Writing the image will take several minutes. Once the write has completed, remove the microSD card from your computer and insert it into your BBB.

Power on the BBB and Android will begin to boot. On the first boot, it will take several minutes for the top-level UI screen to appear. On subsequent boots, it will take only 30 to 60 seconds to reach the top-level UI screen.

Congratulations! Your BBB is now running the Android OS.

Summary

In this chapter, you learned about the hardware that you'll need to develop software for the BeagleBone Black, the electronics components and devices that you will need for the exercises in this book, and how to install an Android distribution onto a microSD card for use on the BBB. In the next chapter, you will learn how Android interacts with hardware at the software level and how the BBB can be configured to interface with the hardware components that you will be using in this book.

2
Interfacing with Android

In the last chapter, you installed Android on your BBB. You also gathered all of the hardware and components that you will need to try out the exercises in this book. Now that you have a working Android system and the hardware needed to explore it, it is time to dive into Android and find out how to prepare it to interface with custom hardware.

Most people would not consider Android and Linux to be very similar, but the two have more in common than you might realize. Underneath the polished UIs and a wide variety of apps, Android is secretly Linux. Android's filesystem layout and services are quite different from those of a typical Linux system, so there are certainly many differences between the two in terms of user space (where apps and other processes execute). In terms of kernel space (where device drivers execute and resources are allocated to each running process), they are almost identical in functionality. Understanding how the BBB interacts with Linux kernel drivers is the key to creating Android apps that can do the same.

In this chapter, we will tell you about Android's hardware abstraction layer, or HAL. We will also introduce you to PacktHAL, a special library that you can include within your apps to interface with hardware on the BBB. We assume that you already have Eclipse **Android Developer Tools (ADT)** with the Android SDK, the Android **Native Development Kit (NDK)**, and the **Android Debug Bridge (ADB)** tools installed and working on your system.

In this chapter, we will cover the following topics:

- Understanding the Android HAL
- Installing PacktHAL
- Setting up the Android NDK for PacktHAL
- Multiplexing the BBB pins

Are you missing a few tools?

If you do not yet have the Eclipse ADT or Android NDK tools installed on your system, you can find installation instructions and download links at these locations:

- **Eclipse ADT**: `http://developer.android.com/sdk`
- **Android NDK**: `http://developer.android.com/tools/sdk/ndk`

How to install ADB is discussed later in this chapter. This chapter assumes that you have installed the Eclipse ADT to the `c:\adt-bundle` directory if you are using Windows (we make no assumptions for Linux) and that you have installed the Android NDK to the `c:\android-ndk` directory (Windows) or `android-ndk` in your home directory (Linux). If you have installed these tools to a different location, you will have to make a few simple adjustments to a few instructions later in this chapter.

Understanding the Android HAL

An Android kernel contains a few additional features that aren't found in a typical Linux kernel, such as **Binder IPC** and the low-memory killer, but otherwise it is still Linux. This provides you with one very big advantage when interfacing hardware with Android, that is, if a Linux driver already exists in the kernel used for an Android system, then you already have an Android driver for that device.

Android apps must interact with the hardware of an Android device by generating video and audio data, receiving button and touchscreen input events, and receiving sensor events from cameras, accelerometers, and other devices that gather information from the outside world. Leveraging existing Linux drivers for these devices makes Android support much easier. Unlike a traditional Linux distribution, which grants applications permission to directly access many different device files (by directly opening files in the `/dev` filesystem), Android dramatically limits the ability of processes to directly access hardware.

Consider the number of different Android apps that use the audio functionality of the device to play sounds or record audio data. Underneath Android, the Linux kernel provides this audio functionality via an **Advanced Linux Sound Architecture** (**ALSA**) audio driver. In most cases, only one process at a time can open and control the ALSA driver resource. If individual apps were in charge of taking, using, and releasing the ALSA driver, it would become a huge mess to coordinate audio resource usage among all of the various apps. One misbehaving app can easily take control of audio resources and block all other apps from using them! But how can the allocation and control of these resources be handled? To solve this problem, Android uses *managers*.

Android managers

Managers are the components of the system that control hardware devices on behalf of all apps. Every app requires some set of resources (such as audio, GPS, and network access) to perform its job. Managers are in charge of allocating and interfacing with each of these resources and determining whether an app has permission to use that resource.

Having managers deal with these low-level details makes life much easier. Android can be installed on a wide variety of hardware platforms that vary wildly in terms of physical size and input/output capabilities, and app developers can't be expected to have intimate knowledge of each and every platform that their app can be installed on.

To use a resource, an app must create a reference to the proper manager via the `getSystemService()` method of the `android.content.Context` class:

```
// Create a reference to the system "location" manager
LocationManager locationManager = (LocationManager)
   mContext.getSystemService(LOCATION_SERVICE);
```

Then, make information and control requests via this manager reference:

```
// Query the location manager to determine if GPS is enabled
isGPSEnabled = locationManager.
isProviderEnabled(LocationManager.GPS_PROVIDER);
```

Apps interact with managers through the Java Android API. While managers respond to these Java methods, they must eventually use the **Java native interface (JNI)** to call the native code that directly interacts with the hardware. This is where the true control of the hardware takes place. The bridge between the Android API and calls to the native code that control the hardware is known as the **hardware abstraction layer (HAL)**.

The various pieces of the HAL are typically written in C/C++, and each device's vendor is responsible for implementing them. If some pieces of the HAL are missing, services and apps won't be able to fully utilize all aspects of the hardware platform. Various Android services use the HAL to communicate with the hardware, and apps use IPC to communicate with these services and gain access to the hardware. The services interact with the hardware on an app's behalf (assuming that the app has the proper Android permissions to access that particular hardware resource).

The HAL development workflow

Typically, creating a complete HAL follows these steps:

1. Identify or develop a Linux kernel device driver to control the hardware.
2. Create a kernel Device Tree overlay that instantiates and configures the driver.
3. Develop a user space library to interface with the kernel device driver.
4. Develop JNI bindings to the userspace library.
5. Develop an Android manager using the JNI bindings to interface with the hardware.

Sometimes, it isn't a clear decision as to where a particular piece of custom hardware should be properly integrated into the HAL and which manager should be in charge of accessing the hardware. What Android permissions control access to the hardware? Will the API have to be extended to offer new types of permissions? Will a custom service have to be created?

Implementing every aspect of a proper HAL for a piece of custom hardware is a bit of an overkill for hobbyists, students, and other developers interested in simple experimentation with hardware interfacing. While a commercial Android system must address all of these steps to develop a proper HAL, we take a far more direct approach to hardware access in this book.

As our focus is on showing how you can interface Android apps with hardware, we skip steps 1 through 4 by providing you with **PacktHAL**, a native library that implements a very simple HAL. PacktHAL will ease you into the daunting task of interfacing with hardware on the BBB, and it provides a set of functions that are capable of interfacing with the hardware used in the examples throughout this book. Strictly speaking, your apps will act as the manager in charge of each hardware resource.

Working with PacktHAL

Apps communicate with the native calls of PacktHAL using JNI. PacktHAL demonstrates how to perform user space interfacing with hardware via three different interfacing methods: GPIO, SPI, and I2C. Using PacktHAL, you have direct access to hardware devices. *Chapters 3* through *Chapter 6* provide examples of how this interfacing works and how you can use it within your own Android app code. Each chapter will examine the various pieces of PacktHAL used in the app examples of that chapter.

How does PacktHAL actually talk to hardware?

Generally, any method that allows you to interface with hardware under Linux can also be used by the HAL for interfacing. Reading, writing, and making `ioctl()` calls to files in the `/dev` filesystem will work, as does using `mmap()` to provide access to memory-mapped control registers. PacktHAL uses all of these techniques to interface with the hardware that you connect to your BBB.

Using PacktHAL is nowhere near as secure as a proper HAL implementation because we must change the permissions on the hardware's user space interfaces such that *any* app can access the hardware directly. This can potentially make your system vulnerable to malicious apps, so such an approach should never be used in a production device. Users that root (gain superuser access to) commercial Android phones and tablets often do so to lessen the strict permissions on these devices by default. This allows them to install and enable custom features, and it provides more flexibility and customization for their devices.

As you are using the BBB as an Android-prototyping device, such an approach is the easiest way for you to interact with the hardware. This is a stepping stone towards developing your own custom managers and services that speak to your hardware on behalf of apps. Ideally, on a commercial device, only an Android manager will have the necessary permissions to directly interface with the hardware.

Once you become comfortable with using PacktHAL in your apps, you can then examine PacktHAL's source code to better understand how native code interfaces with the Linux kernel. Eventually, you might find yourself integrating PacktHAL into your own custom managers. You might even find yourself developing custom code for the actual kernel!

Installing PacktHAL

All of the various pieces of PacktHAL are located in the `PacktHAL.tgz` file, which is available for download from Packt's website (`http://www.packtpub.com/support`). This is a compressed tar file that contains all of the source code and configuration files required to modify BBBAndroid to use PacktHAL and include PacktHAL support in your apps.

Preparing PacktHAL under Linux

Once you have downloaded the `PacktHAL.tgz` file, you must decompress and untar it. We will assume that you have copied `PacktHAL.tgz` to your home directory after downloading it and will decompress it from there. We will refer to your home directory as `$HOME`.

Use the Linux `tar` command to decompress and untar the file:

```
$ cd $HOME
$ tar -xvf PacktHAL.tgz
```

A directory named `PacktHAL` now exists in your `$HOME` directory. All of the PacktHAL files are located in this directory.

Preparing PacktHAL under Windows

Once you have downloaded the `PacktHAL.tgz` file, decompress and untar it. We will assume that you have copied `PacktHAL.tgz` to the root directory of the `C:` drive after downloading it and will use WinRAR to decompress it from there.

Where should I unpack PacktHAL.tgz?

You can decompress and untar `PacktHAL.tgz` on the desktop or wherever else you wish, but you will be performing some command-line commands to copy files around later. It is much simpler to perform these operations if `PacktHAL.tgz` is decompressed and untarred in the root directory of the `C:` drive, so we will assume that you are performing these operations from there.

Perform the following steps to extract the `PacktHAL.tgz` file:

1. Open a file explorer window and navigate to the root of the `C:` drive.
2. Right-click on the `PacktHAL.tgz` file in file explorer and select **Extract Here**.

A directory named `C:\PacktHAL` now exists. All of the PacktHAL files are located in this directory.

The PacktHAL directory structure

The PacktHAL directory has the following structure:

```
PacktHAL/
    |
    +----cape/
    |       |
    |       +----BB-PACKTPUB-00A0.dts
    |       +----build_cape.sh
    |
    +----jni/
    |       |
    |       +----(Various .c and .h files)
    |       +----(Various .mk files)
    |
    +----prebuilt/
    |       |
    |       +----BB-PACTPUB-00A0.dtbo
    |       +----init.genericam33xx(flatteneddevicetr.rc
    |       +----spi
    |           |
    |               +----spidev.h
    |
    +----README.txt
```

The cape subdirectory contains the source code and build script for building a Device Tree overlay that enables all of the hardware features that PacktHAL needs. You will learn more about Device Tree overlays later in this chapter. The jni subdirectory contains the source code files that implement PacktHAL. These source files will be added to your projects in later chapters to build PacktHAL support into your apps. The prebuilt directory contains a few premade files that must be added to your BBBAndroid image and Android NDK to build and use PacktHAL. You will install the files in the prebuilt directory to their required locations in the next few sections.

Preparing Android for PacktHAL

Before using PacktHAL with any apps, you have to prepare your BBBAndroid installation. By default, Android is very restrictive on the permissions that it assigns to hardware devices. To use PacktHAL, you must lessen the permission restrictions and configure Android for the hardware that you will interface with. These actions require copying some prebuilt files into your Android system to make a few configuration changes that relax various Android permissions and configure the hardware properly for PacktHAL's use.

You will use the ADB tool to push (push) the necessary files over to your running BBB system. Prior to pushing the files, boot Android on the BBB and connect the BBB to your PC using the USB cable that came with your BBB. Once you have reached this point, continue with the instructions.

Pushing PacktHAL files under Linux

The following steps are used in order to publish PacktHAL files under Linux:

1. Before you get started, make sure that ADB can see your BBB by using the adb devices command. The BBB will report as having a serial number of BBBAndroid. Execute the following command:

    ```
    $ adb devices
    List of devices attached
    BBBAndroid        device
    ```

2. If you are missing the adb command, install the android-tools-adb package via apt-get:

    ```
    $ sudo apt-get install android-tools-adb
    ```

Why can't Linux find my BBB?

If adb is installed on your system and you are unable to see the BBB, you might need to add a udev rule to your system and perform some additional troubleshooting. Google provides directions for adding this rule and some troubleshooting steps if you run into any difficulty, and this can be found at http://developer.android.com/tools/device.html.

BBBAndroid reports the USB device ID of its ADB interface as 18D1:4E23, which is the device ID of a Google Nexus S, so the USB vendor ID for the BBB is 18D1 (the device ID for Google devices).

3. Once you have verified that adb can see the BBB, change into the PacktHAL directory, shell into Android via adb, and remount the read-only rootfs filesystem as read-write:

    ```
    $ cd $HOME/PacktHAL/prebuilt
    $ adb shell
    root@beagleboneblack:/ # mount rootfs rootfs / rw
    root@beagleboneblack:/ # exit
    ```

4. Now, push the necessary files into Android's `rootfs` filesystem:

```
$ adb push BB-PACKTPUB-00A0.dtbo /system/vendor/firmware
$ adb push init.genericam33xx\(flatteneddevicetr.rc /
$ adb chmod 750 /init.genericam33xx\(flatteneddevicetr.rc
```

5. Finally, shell into Android's `rootfs` filesystem to sync it and remount it as read-only:

```
$ adb shell
root@beagleboneblack:/ # sync
root@beagleboneblack:/ # mount rootfs rootfs / ro remount
root@beagleboneblack:/ # exit
```

6. You have now prepared your BBBAndroid image for PacktHAL under Linux. Remove the power supply cable and USB cable from your BBB to shut it down.

7. Then, power up the BBB to verify that Android boots properly with the modifications that you have just made.

Pushing PacktHAL files under Windows

You must locate where your `adb.exe` file is located. It is part of the platform tools in the Android SDK. In the following instructions, we are assuming that you installed the Eclipse ADT in the `c:\adt-bundle` directory, making the full path to `adb` to be `c:\adt-bundle\sdk\platform-tools\adb.exe`.

The following steps are used in order to publish PacktHAL files under Windows:

1. Before you get started, make sure that `adb` can see your BBB by using the `adb devices` command. The BBB will report as having a serial number of BBBAndroid:

```
$ adb devices
List of devices attached
BBBAndroid      device
```

Why can't Windows find my BBB?

It can be notoriously difficult to get `adb` to see Android devices under Windows. This is because each hardware manufacturer that creates an Android device provides its own Windows ADB device driver that Windows uses to talk to that device. BBBAndroid reports the USB device ID of its ADB interface as `18D1:4E23`, which is the device ID of a Google Nexus S. This device is one of the (many) USB devices that are supported by Koushik Dutta's excellent Universal ADB driver for Windows. If `adb` can't find your BBB, install the Universal ADB driver and then try again. You can download the driver from `http://www.koushikdutta.com/post/universal-adb-driver`.

2. Once you have verified this, `adb` can see the BBB, shell into Android via `adb`, and remount the read-only `rootfs` filesystem as read-write:

```
$ adb shell
root@beagleboneblack:/ # mount rootfs rootfs / rw
root@beagleboneblack:/ # exit
```

3. Now, push the necessary files into Android's `rootfs` filesystem:

```
$ adb push c:\PacktHAL\prebuilt\BB-PACKTPUB-00A0.dtbo /system/vendor/firmware
$ adb push c:\PacktHAL\prebuilt\init.
genericam33xx(flatteneddevicetr.rc /
$ adb chmod 750 /init.genericam33xx\flatteneddevicetr.rc
```

4. Finally, shell into Android's `rootfs` filesystem to sync it and remount it as read-only:

```
$ adb shell
root@beagleboneblack:/ # sync
root@beagleboneblack:/ # mount rootfs rootfs / ro remount
root@beagleboneblack:/ # exit
```

5. You have now prepared your BBBAndroid image for PacktHAL under Windows. Remove the power supply cable and USB cable from your BBB to shut it down. Then, power up the BBB to verify that Android boots properly with the modifications that you have just made.

Why is it that the init.genericam33xx(flatteneddevicetr.rc file is named so oddly?

Android devices have a set of read-only properties that describe the hardware and software of the system to apps and managers. One of these properties is `ro.hardware`, which describes the hardware that the kernel is configured for. Device-specific `.rc` files in Android have the `init.{ro.hardware}.*rc` form.

In the Linux kernel source, the `arch/arm/mach-omap2/board-generic.c` file uses a `DT_MACHINE_START()` macro to specify the name of the BBB platform as `Generic AM33XX (Flattened Device Tree)`. This text string is converted to lowercase, spaces are removed, and the string is truncated to produce the final string that is stored in the `ro.hardware` property.

Setting up the Android NDK for PacktHAL

Unfortunately, the Android **Native Development Kit** (**NDK**) is missing a kernel header file that is needed to build PacktHAL. The missing header describes the interface between user space apps and the generic SPI driver (`spidev`, which you will use in *Chapter 5, Interfacing with High-speed Sensors Using SPI*). It is not the fault of the NDK that this header file is missing, as usually apps will never need direct access to the `spidev` driver.

As you are using an app to talk directly talk to the hardware, you will need to copy this missing header into your NDK installation.

For your convenience, we have included a copy of this header file in the PacktHAL source tarball. You only need to copy the file into your NDK installation prior to building PacktHAL.

BBBAndroid is 4.4.4 KitKat, and API level 19 is the highest level supported by this version. You will be building all of the examples in this book for API level 19. Each API level has a different set of headers in the NDK, so you must add the missing headers to the `include/linux` directory for API level 19. If you decide to build apps at lower API levels, you can repeat the following steps to add the additional header file to any of the other API levels that you wish to.

Adding the header to the NDK under Linux

If you are going to be building apps using Eclipse ADT under Linux, you will need to have the Android NDK installed on your Linux system. For these instructions, we will assume that you have already installed the NDK to the `android-ndk` folder in your `$HOME` directory. As you have already downloaded, decompressed, and untarred the `PacktHAL.tgz` file to your `$HOME` directory earlier in this chapter, we will assume that the `PacktHAL` directory that you created is still there:

```
$ cd $HOME/android-ndk/platforms/android-19/arch-arm/usr/include/linux
$ cp -rf $HOME/PacktHAL/prebuilt/spi
```

This will copy the contents of the `spi` header file directory into your NDK header files. Your Linux NDK installation now has the extra header file that it needs to build PacktHAL.

Adding the header to the NDK under Windows

If you are going to be building apps using Eclipse ADT under Windows, you will need to have the Android NDK installed on your Windows system. For these instructions, we will assume that you have installed the NDK to the `c:\android-ndk` folder. As you have already downloaded, decompressed, and untarred the `PacktHAL.tgz` file to your `c:\` directory earlier in this chapter, we will assume that the `PacktHAL` directory that you created is still there:

1. Open a file explorer window and navigate to the `c:\android-ndk\platforms\android-19\arch-arm\usr\include\linux` path.
2. Open a second file explorer window and navigate to the `c:\PacktHAL\prebuilt` path. Right-click on the `spi` directory and select **Copy** from the context menu.
3. Change to the Android NDK window, right-click anywhere within the white space of the file list in the window, and select **Paste** from the context menu.

This will copy the contents of the `spi` header file directory into your NDK header files. Your Windows NDK installation now has the extra header file that it needs to build PacktHAL.

Multiplexing the BBB pins

As accessing hardware resources follows the same process under Android as it does under Linux, it is important to understand how the Linux kernel configures device drivers and allocates them to particular pieces of hardware. It is also necessary to understand how these kernel drivers provide user space interfaces that PacktHAL can interact with.

The BBB's AM3359 processor offers a wide variety of signals on its hundreds of pins. These signals include many different, specialized interface buses and sensor inputs. There are far too many potential signals for the number of pins available to supply these signals to the outside world. To select which signals are available on the pins, the pins are multiplexed, or *muxed*, to specific signals.

Several of the processor's pins are wired to the connections of the BBB's P8 and P9 headers. The muxing of these particular pins is of great interest to BBB users, as the muxing determines which processor signals and features are easily accessible to the user for hardware interfacing. There are 46 pins on each of the BBB's two headers, giving you a total of 92 pins to interface with. Unfortunately, 61 of these pins are in use by default, meaning that only 31 pins can be changed around for your projects without you having to disable one or more standard features of the BBB to make more pins available.

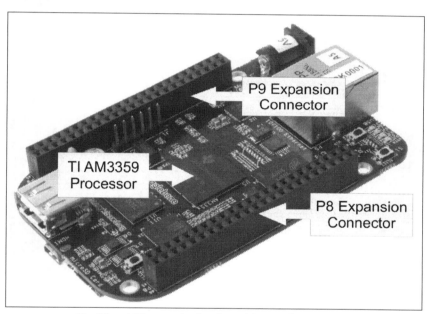

The P8 and P9 expansion headers of the BeagleBone Black

Some pins on the headers are permanently assigned, such as the pins that provide access to voltage (1.8, 3.3, and 5 VDC are available) and ground signals. The other pins though, can be muxed to meet the needs of your project. Proper muxing all of the P8/P9 pins to provide all of the resources that you require can sometimes be tricky, particularly if you are only beginning to learn about the hardware interfacing aspects of the BBB. Luckily, we have already determined a pinmux configuration for you that will provide PacktHAL with all of the hardware resources that it needs to run all of the exercises in this book.

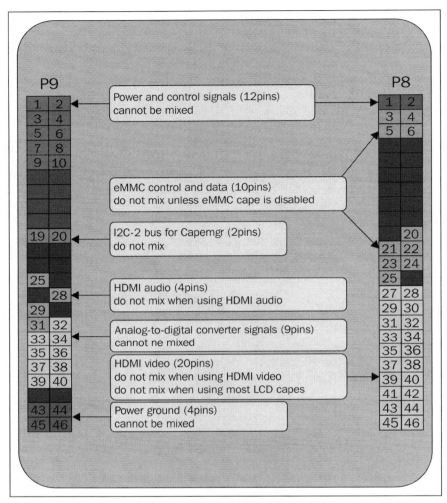

Default pins in use on the BeagleBone Black

The kernel Device Tree and capemgr

The pins of the BBB must be muxed in a specific way to speak with custom hardware, but where and how is this actually done? The answer is "the kernel's **Device Tree**." The Device Tree is a hierarchical data structure inside the kernel that describes what hardware is present, which resources are used by that hardware, and which kernel drivers should be used to talk to each hardware device. It describes different facets of the hardware, such as pin muxing settings, clock speeds, and parameters that are passed to kernel device drivers.

It would be an annoying hassle if the user was required to install a new kernel every time the hardware changed. For a hardware platform like the BBB, the user can change the hardware connected to the BBB between power cycles! It would be very useful to be able to dynamically change the Device Tree to add or remove hardware on the fly. The BBB's Linux 3.8 kernel has a special subsystem, called the **cape manager** (**capemgr**) that allows you to do just that.

The capemgr dynamically adds and removes pieces or *overlays* of the Device Tree. It provides three important services:

- It recognizes any cape hardware that is connected to the BBB
- It loads the appropriate Device Tree overlay to enable and configure each recognized cape
- It allows arbitrary Device Tree overlays to be loaded dynamically from user space to configure any hardware that is not automatically discovered

Defining a cape

A cape is any hardware add-on that connects to the BBB's P8/P9 connectors (similar to how shield boards connect to an Arduino) and contains an **electrically erasable programmable read-only memory** (**EEPROM**) chip that reports the cape's identity to the kernel's capebus. The capemgr in the kernel can then dynamically enable the appropriate Device Tree overlay for that particular cape. This is what allows you to connect a variety of different, commercially available cape boards to the BBB, and they all just automatically work without you having to change a single configuration file.

A much looser definition of a cape is any external circuitry that interfaces via the P8/P9 connectors. Without including an EEPROM that tells the capemgr "I am a cape and my name is XYZ", the capemgr won't automatically locate and load the proper Device Tree overlay for the cape. This is the case for all of the examples in this book. You can still consider the hardware that you connect to the BBB to be a cape that Android is interfacing with, but the Device Tree overlay must be loaded manually from user space.

Earlier in this chapter, you used `adb` to push a file named `BB-PACKTPUB-00A0.dtbo` to your Android image. This file is the Device Tree overlay that configures the BBB for the hardware that you will use in the exercises throughout this book. The custom `init.genericam33xx(flatteneddevicetr.rc` file that you also pushed over to the Android image manually loads this overlay for you during Android's boot process.

In the Linux filesystem, custom overlays are placed into the `/lib/firmware` directory. Under Android, however, there is no `/lib` directory in `rootfs`, so overlays are instead placed into the `/system/vendor/firmware` directory. This is also the location where firmware (`.fw` files) built during kernel compilation is installed. When using your own Device Tree overlays for your future projects, remember to place them into the `/system/vendor/firmware` directory so that the capemgr can find them.

Where can I learn more about multiplexing the BBB's pins, the Device Tree, and creating custom overlays?

Learning how to select the best pin muxing for custom projects and creating the appropriate Device Tree overlays are outside the scope of this book, but there are many excellent resources available that can introduce you to the process. Here are a few great resources we recommend that you read to learn more:

- The BeagleBone Black System reference manual: `http://www.adafruit.com/datasheets/BBB_SRM.pdf`

- Derek Molloy's website: `http://derekmolloy.ie/category/embedded-systems/beaglebone/`

- AdaFruit's Device Tree Overlay tutorial: `https://learn.adafruit.com/introduction-to-the-beaglebone-black-device-tree`

Summary

In this chapter, we explained how Android uses a HAL to allow Android managers to provide hardware access to apps. We introduced you to PacktHAL that can be used to interface with all of the examples throughout this book. You configured your BBBAndroid image to use PacktHAL, and you modified your NDK installation to build PacktHAL into your apps.

We also showed which pins of the BBB's P8/P9 headers can be multiplexed, what the Device Tree is and how it is used to multiplex pins, and how the capemgr loads Device Tree overlays to dynamically mux the BBB's pins.

In the next chapter, you'll put PacktHAL to work and build your first hardware-interfacing app using GPIOs.

3
Handling Inputs and Outputs with GPIOs

In the last chapter, you prepared your development PC and BBBAndroid system for the development of hardware-interfacing Android apps. Now that your development environment is set up and ready to go, you will begin exploring your very first app that is capable of direct communication with hardware connected to the BBB.

General-Purpose Input/Output (GPIO) is one of the most basic interfaces in digital electronics. In the examples within this chapter, you will be working with GPIOs to receive digital input signals from the outside world and send digital output signals back in response. While this is a small start, it is the first step in developing and understanding hardware-interfacing apps that are much more complex. GPIOs can be used to implement complex and powerful interfacing logic. We will discuss both the hardware and software sides of GPIO interfacing and explain how calling Java methods in Android apps can interface with low-level hardware-interfacing code.

In this chapter, we will cover the following topics:

- Understanding GPIOs
- Building a GPIO interface circuit
- Including PacktHAL within your apps
- Exploring the GPIO example app

Understanding GPIOs

At its most basic level, communication between two pieces of hardware requires the transmission of data back and forth between them. In computer systems, this data is represented as voltage levels sent over a wire that connects the devices together. The patterns and levels of voltage back and forth form a communication protocol that the devices use to transmit data between each other.

GPIO is the most basic interfacing option offered by microcontrollers and microprocessors. Some pins of the BBB's processor are allocated as GPIOs that act as an *input* (monitoring voltage on the wire to receive data) or an *output* (placing a particular voltage on the wire to send data). The BBB has dozens of available GPIO pins, which makes GPIO a flexible and simple way for Android apps to interact with the outside world without requiring fancy device drivers or extra interfacing hardware.

Nuts and bolts of GPIO

Digital logic operates on the concept that there are two discrete voltage levels that represent an *on/high* state and an *off/low* state. By toggling between these two states, binary bits of data are transmitted between devices. The BBB uses the voltage of 3.3 V for its high level and a voltage of 0 V (connected to a ground) for the low level. This voltage scheme is known as a *3.3 V logic level*, and it is commonly used for single-board computers such as the BeagleBoard and Raspberry Pi. Many microcontrollers (many Arduinos, for example) use a 5 V logic level instead.

Never apply more than 3.3 V to any BBB pin!

Applying greater than 3.3 V to a BBB GPIO can fry the BBB's processor, so always make sure that you only work with a maximum of 3.3 V when designing the GPIO interface circuitry for the BBB. Pins P9.3/4 supply 3.3 V, and pins P9.5/6 supply 5 V. It is very simple to accidentally connect a breadboard wire to the pins supplying 5 V when you intended to use the 3.3 V pins. To help avoid this mistake, try covering the P9.5/6 pins with a piece of tape. This prevents you from accidentally inserting a breadboard wire into these pins.

The BBB's processor has four banks of GPIOs, with 32 individual GPIOs in each bank. With only 92 pins available on the P8/9 connectors, it is not possible to give every GPIO access to the outside world. In fact, the BBB's System Reference Manual shows that it is only possible to mux about 65 unique GPIOs to P8/P9 at the same time, even if every other feature being muxed to P8/9 was disabled. There are a few other GPIOs that are used internally for tasks such as lighting and blinking the BBB's LEDs, but you should consider yourself restricted to only using the GPIOs that are accessible via P8/P9 and that do not conflict with any of the standard BBB features.

GPIO access methods under Android

There are two basic approaches to interacting with GPIOs on the BBB: **file I/O** and **memory-mapping**. With the file I/O, you pass GPIO requests through a kernel driver by reading and writing to GPIO files in the filesystem. With memory-mapping, you map the GPIO control resistors into memory and then read and write these mapped memory locations to directly manipulate the control resistors. As both of these methods are made possible by the Linux kernel, they will both work just as well under Android as they do under Linux.

Pros and cons of the file I/O method

The file I/O method can be performed by any process that has the proper permissions to read/write the GPIO device files. However, like any file I/O operation, this can be quite slow.

Pros and cons of the memory-mapping method

The memory-mapping method allows you to directly access the resistors that control the GPIOs. Memory-mapping is very fast (about 1000 times faster than file I/O!), but only processes with root permissions can use it.

As your apps are unable to execute with root permissions without some serious permission changes, you will be unable to use memory-mapping to access GPIOs. This effectively restricts you to only using file I/O for your apps.

> PacktHAL implements both memory-mapping and file I/O for GPIO access. If you are interested in the low-level details of how both of these approaches work, examine the `jni/gpio.c` file in `PacktHAL.tgz`.

Preparing Android for GPIO use

In *Chapter 2, Interfacing with Android*, you used `adb` to push two prebuilt files from PacktHAL to your Android system. These two files, `BB-PACKTPUB-00A0.dtbo` and `init.{ro.hardware}.rc`, configure your Android system to enable specific GPIOs and allow your apps to access them.

> Remember that when we talk about the `init.{ro.hardware}.rc` file, we are referring to the `init.genericam33xx(flatteneddevice.tr` file in the root directory of the Android filesystem.

The BB-PACKTPUB-00A0.dtbo file is a Device Tree overlay that muxes the BBB to support all of the examples in this book. As far as GPIOs are concerned, this overlay muxes the P9.11 and P9.13 pins into GPIOs. In the PacktHAL.tgz file, the source code for the overlay is located in the cape/BB-PACKTPUB-00A0.dts file. The code responsible for muxing the two GPIOs is located in the bb_gpio_pins node within fragment@0:

```
/* All GPIO pins are PULLUP, MODE7 */
bb_gpio_pins: pinmux_bb_gpio_pins {
    pinctrl-single,pins = <
        0x070 0x17  /* P9.11, gpio0_30, OUTPUT */
        0x074 0x37  /* P9.13, gpio0_31, INPUT */
    >;
};
```

The details of the hex values used in the bb_gpio_pins node are beyond the scope of this book. However, the general idea is that they specify which pin is of interest, which mode the pin should be muxed to, a few details about pull-up/pull-down resistors, whether it is an input or an output pin, and whether any skewing adjustments should be made to the signal.

 The details of what skew is and how to adjust for it are beyond the scope of this book. If you would like to learn more about skewing, we suggest the Wikipedia page on the subject as a good starting point (http://en.wikipedia.org/wiki/Clock_skew).

At boot, this overlay is loaded by the init.{ro.hardware}.rc file. The kernel then knows which pins are treated as GPIOs. After loading the overlay, the init.{ro.hardware}.rc file then executes a few commands that explicitly "unlock" these GPIO files for use by apps by *exporting* them. Exporting a GPIO pin creates a series of files in the /sys filesystem that can be read and written to interact with that GPIO pin.

By exporting a GPIO pin and then changing the permissions of the proper files in the /sys filesystem via chmod, any process can read from or write to GPIOs. This is exactly what the commands in the init.{ro.hardware}.rc file do to allow Android apps to interface with GPIOs. The following portion of the init.{ro.hardware}.rc file performs the export and chmod operations:

```
# Export GPIOs 30 and 31 (P9.11 and P9.13)
write /sys/class/gpio/export 30
write /sys/class/gpio/export 31

# Make GPIO 30 an output
write /sys/class/gpio/gpio30/direction out
```

```
# Make GPIOs 30 and 31 writeable from the FS
chmod 777 /sys/class/gpio/gpio30/value
chmod 777 /sys/class/gpio/gpio31/value
```

Each GPIO has a specific integer identifier that is determined by the bank the GPIO belongs to and its position within that bank. In our case, the GPIO muxed to P9.11 is the 30th GPIO in bank 0, and P9.13 is the 31st GPIO in bank 0. This makes their integer identifiers 30 and 31, respectively.

 The GPIO pins 30 and 31 are only available via the /sys filesystem because they were explicitly exported via the write commands in the init. {ro.hardware}.rc file. Other GPIO pins will not be available via the filesystem unless they are also explicitly exported in the same fashion.

This is a very insecure way of allowing GPIO access because it opens up the GPIOs for use by processes that we might not want to have direct access to them. For experimentation and prototyping, this is not a problem. However, you certainly should not do this in a commercial system. Unless you develop a proper, privileged Android manager to handle the GPIO resources, you must allow *all* processes to access the GPIO files unless you tailor the permissions to only be usable by apps belonging to a specific user or group. As each app is assigned its own user, you would have to chown the GPIOs to the proper user and group after you install the app's .apk file onto the system.

Building a GPIO-interfacing circuit

Before you begin developing software that communicates using GPIOs, you must first construct a hardware circuit for the GPIOs to interface with. For this chapter, you will build a simple circuit that consists of a 1k ohm resistor, an LED, and a pushbutton switch. Part numbers and suppliers for these components were listed in *Chapter 1, Introduction to Android and the BeagleBone Black*. Before getting started, be sure that you have all of the proper parts and remove all power sources from your BBB (unplug the power supply and USB cables) prior to connecting anything to the BBB's P8/P9 connector.

 Don't disassemble your circuit!

The GPIO circuit in this chapter is part of a much larger circuit used in *Chapter 6, Creating a Complete Interfacing Solution*. If you build the circuit as it is positioned in the following diagram (towards the top of the breadboard), you can simply leave the GPIO components and wires in place as you build the remaining circuits in this book. This way, it will already be constructed and working when you reach *Chapter 6*.

Constructing the circuit

The circuit that you will build interfaces with the following four BBB's pins:

- P9.1 (ground)
- P9.3 (3.3 V)
- P9.11 (GPIO)
- P9.13 (GPIO)

The P9.11 pin is configured as an output GPIO, and it drives the LED. The P9.13 pin is configured as an input GPIO, and it sets its state depending upon the input voltage that is applied to it. Both GPIO pins are configured by the BB-PACKTPUB-00A0.dtbo overlay to use an internal pull-up resistor. If you are not familiar with what a pull-up resistor is, don't worry. For the purposes of these examples, it simply means that the logic level of the GPIOs will not "float" between on and off if nothing is attached to the GPIO pins. Instead, the logic level will be "pulled-up" to the on state.

 Interested in learning more about what a pull-up resistor is and how it works? We suggest that you check out this online tutorial on pull-up and pull-down resistors, available at http://www.resistorguide.com/pull-up-resistor_pull-down-resistor.

Breadboards typically have two vertical buses on either side that run almost the entire length of the breadboard. These buses are used to provide convenient access to power and ground signals for any components inserted into the breadboard.

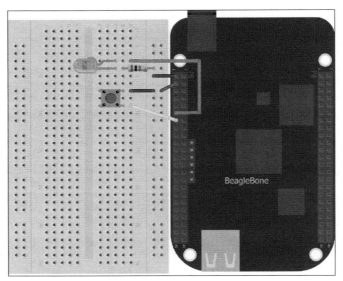

The complete GPIO-interfacing circuit

Now we can start constructing our circuit:

1. Connect the BBB's ground (P9.1) and 3.3 V (P9.3) signals to the two vertical buses on the breadboard. The ground bus is the vertical bus towards the center of the breadboard. The 3.3 V bus is the vertical bus towards the edge of the breadboard.

2. Next, connect the anode, or the positive lead, of the LED to P9.11. LEDs have a polarity, so current will only flow through them in one direction. Current flows from the longer lead (the anode) of the LED to the shorter lead (the cathode).

3. If the LED's leads have been cut to the same length and you are unable to tell which lead is which, feel around the edge of the LED's plastic casing. The edge of the casing is flat on the cathode side and rounded on the anode side. As long as the cathode is connected to the ground and the anode is connected to the GPIO pin, the LED will work properly.

4. You must limit the current drawn by the LED to ensure that you do not damage the GPIO pin, so place a 1K ohm resistor between the LED's cathode lead and the ground signal. Resistors do not have a polarity like LEDs do, so the direction that you connect it to the breadboard will not matter.

> If you wish to learn more about using a current-limiting resistor with an LED, such as selecting the right resistor for the task, we suggest that you read the tutorial from SparkFun, available at https://www.sparkfun.com/tutorials/219.

5. Now that the LED and resistor have been connected to the BBB, you must connect the pushbutton switch. Different switches have different numbers of leads, but the switch that we suggested for your use has a total of four leads. These leads form two pairs of two leads each. The two leads in each pair are always electrically connected to each other, but one pair will only be electrically connected to the other pair when the button is being pressed. Two sides of the switch are smooth, and the other two sides have two protruding leads on each side. The two protruding leads on a single side of the switch belong to different pairs of leads. Pick one side of the switch with two leads on it and connect one lead to P9.13 and the other lead to the breadboard's ground bus.

Your circuit is now complete. Double-check your wiring against the diagram of the complete GPIO-interfacing circuit to ensure that everything is connected properly.

Checking your wiring

Once you have completed the wiring of the GPIO circuit, you should test it to ensure that it works properly. Luckily, you can do this easily by shelling into the BBB and working with the exported GPIO pin files. We will assume that you are using `adb` to shell into the Android system, but using the FTDI to access the console shell will work in exactly the same way.

How do I use the FTDI cable?

If you have never used an FTDI cable to communicate with your BBB, there is a page on the www.elinux.org wiki (maintained by the BeagleBoard.org staff) that can help you get started, which is http://elinux.org/Beagleboard:Terminal_Shells.

In this book, we will only be using the USB cable and ADB shell to access the BBB. However, learning how to use the FTDI to monitor and troubleshoot your BBB can really come in handy.

Connect power to your BBB and then use the USB cable to connect the BBB to your development system. After shelling into the BBB, begin testing your GPIO circuit using the following steps:

1. Change into the directory for the GPIO pin muxed to P9.11 (GPIO pin 30):

   ```
   root@beagleboneblack:/ # cd /sys/class/gpio/gpio30
   ```

2. Use the `echo` command to turn the LED on by forcing the state of this GPIO to 1:

   ```
   root@beagleboneblack:/ # echo 1 > value
   ```

3. The LED will now be turned on. Use the `echo` command to turn the LED off by forcing the state of this GPIO to 0:

   ```
   root@beagleboneblack:/ # echo 0 > value
   ```

4. The LED will now be turned off. Change into the directory for the GPIO pin muxed to P9.13 (the GPIO pin 31):

   ```
   root@beagleboneblack:/ # cd /sys/class/gpio/gpio31
   ```

5. Use the `cat` command to check the current state of the pushbutton switch. When executing this command, make sure that you are not pushing the button:

   ```
   root@beagleboneBlack:/ # cat value
   1
   ```

6. Now, execute the following `cat` command while holding down the button. You should type the entire command, press the button, and then hit the *Enter* key to enter the command while still holding the button down:

```
root@beagleboneblack:/ # cat value
0
```

> The pushbutton values look reversed because of how the circuit is wired. The pull-up resistor on P9.13 will pull the value of the GPIO to `1` when the button is not pressed. When the button is pressed, the P9.13 pin becomes connected to the ground signal and changes the GPIO to `0`.

If you saw the LED turn on and off and the correct values were returned when the switch was pressed and released, you have correctly wired the circuit. If the LED did not light up, make sure that you have not accidentally swapped the anode and cathode leads of the LED. If the switch always returns a value of 0, make sure that you have connected the correct pair of leads on the switch to the ground signal bus and P9.13.

Including PacktHAL within your apps

Before diving into using PacktHAL to interface with GPIOs, you must understand how to include PacktHAL support in your apps. We will walk you through the process of adding the PacktHAL code into your app and then building it. PacktHAL will be packaged with your app in the `.apk` app as a shared library. The source code for the library exists within the app's project directory, but it is built separately from the Java code of the app. You must manually build the PacktHAL shared library before your app can include it within the `.apk` app and use it.

> We include a prebuilt version of the PacktHAL library in each of the example app projects included with this book, so you can jump into building and running the example apps right away without worrying about the details of building PacktHAL. Once you begin creating your own custom apps and modifying PacktHAL for your own hardware projects, you will need to understand how to build PacktHAL from source.

Understanding the Java Native Interface

Android apps are written in Java, but the functions in PacktHAL are written in C native code. Native code is the code that is compiled into a native binary, such as a shared library or executable, and then executed directly by the Android OS. Native code is built using the compiler toolchain supplied within the Android NDK. Native binaries are not as portable as the "build once, run anywhere" bytecode of Android apps, but they can be used for low-level interfacing in ways that Java code cannot. Unlike Java bytecode, which is executable on any platform that has a proper virtual machine, native code is compiled for one specific hardware architecture (such as ARM, x86, or PowerPC) and can be executed only on that architecture.

Functions implemented in native code are called from an app's Java code via the **Java Native Interface (JNI)**. JNI is a popular interfacing mechanism that Java applications use to interact with native C/C++ code. Among other features, JNI is used to *translate* Java datatypes into C datatypes and vice versa.

For example, consider the Java `String` type. While Java has a `String` implementation, there is no equivalent type in C. The string must be suitably converted to a compatible type before it can be used by the C code. Each Java type is represented in C by a series of equivalent types, such as `jint`, `jstring`, and `jboolean`, which are defined in the standard `jni.h` header file that is supplied by the Android NDK.

Creating a new app project that uses PacktHAL

The following steps demonstrate how you can create a new custom app that includes PacktHAL:

1. Launch the Eclipse ADT and select the menu option **File**, then **New**, then **Android Application Project**.

2. In the **New Android Application** dialog, enter `myapp` into the **Application Name** field. This will automatically populate the **Project Name** and **Application Name** fields. Change the **Minimum Required SDK**, **Target SDK**, and **Compile With** fields to **API 19: Android 4.4**. The theme field can be left alone or changed to whichever theme you would like for your app. When finished, click on the **Next** button.

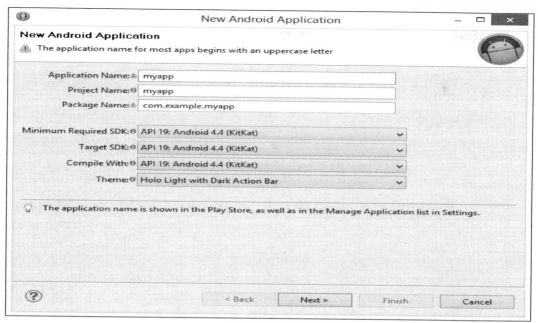

The New Android Application screen

3. Proceed through the successive dialog screens, retaining the default settings for each screen, until you click on the **Finish** button on the final screen.

The name of the default activity created for your new app is MainActivity. After creating the new project, the folder structure of your new myapp project will reside in the myapp ($PROJECT) directory and have a directory structure similar to the following:

```
myapp
  |
  +----.settings/
  +----assets/
  +----bin/
  +----gen/
  +----libs/
  +----res/
  +----src/
  +----...
```

After creating the app for the first time, several new folders will be created to hold the various intermediary files created during the build process. Once you have created your app, you must add the PacktHAL code to it and compile it.

Building PacktHAL under Windows

PacktHAL must be built into a library and included within your app's project codebase to be used by your app. Assuming that you decompressed and untarred the PacktHAL.tgz file in c:\, you can copy the PacktHAL code into your app's project directory ($PROJECT) using the following process:

1. Open a file explorer window and browse to the $PROJECT directory.

2. Open a second file explorer window and browse to c:\PacktHAL.

3. Right-click on the jni directory in the c:\PacktHAL directory and select **Copy** from the context menu.

4. Right-click anywhere convenient on white space within the $PROJECT directory window and then select **Paste** from the context menu.

Now that the jni\ directory exists in your $PROJECT directory, you can build PacktHAL using the Android NDK. Assuming that you installed the Android NDK in c:\android-ndk, you can build PacktHAL using the following process:

1. Launch cmd.exe for a command prompt window. Using the command prompt, change into the $PROJECT directory:

   ```
   c:\> cd $PROJECT\jni
   ```

2. Build the PacktHAL library using the Android NDK:

   ```
   c:\$PROJECT\jni> c:\android-ndk\ndk-build

   [armeabi] Compile thumb  : packtHAL <= jni_wrapper.c

   [armeabi] Compile thumb  : packtHAL <= gpio.c

   [armeabi] Compile thumb  : packtHAL <= fram.c

   [armeabi] Compile thumb  : packtHAL <= bmp183.c

   [armeabi] SharedLibrary  : libpacktHAL.so

   [armeabi] Install        : libpacktHAL.so => libs/armeabi/
   libpacktHAL.so
   ```

The PacktHAL library is now built and present in your project as the file $PROJECT\
libs\armeabi\libpacktHAL.so.

Building PacktHAL under Linux

PacktHAL must be built into a library and included within your app's project codebase to be used by your app. Assuming that you decompressed and untarred the `PacktHAL.tgz` file in your `$HOME` directory, you can copy the PacktHAL code into your app's project directory (`$PROJECT`) using the following commands:

```
$ cd $PROJECT
$ cp -rf $HOME/PacktHAL/jni .
```

Now that the `jni` directory exists in your `$PROJECT` directory, you can build PacktHAL using the Android NDK. Assuming that you installed the Android NDK in `$HOME/android-ndk`, you can build PacktHAL using the following process:

1. Change into the `$PROJECT/jni` directory:

   ```
   $ cd $PROJECT/jni
   ```

2. Build the PacktHAL library using the Android NDK:

   ```
   $ ./$HOME/android-ndk/ndk-build
   [armeabi] Compile thumb  : packtHAL <= jni_wrapper.c
   [armeabi] Compile thumb  : packtHAL <= gpio.c
   [armeabi] Compile thumb  : packtHAL <= fram.c
   [armeabi] Compile thumb  : packtHAL <= bmp183.c
   [armeabi] SharedLibrary  : libpacktHAL.so
   [armeabi] Install        : libpacktHAL.so => libs/armeabi/
   libpacktHAL.so
   ```

The PacktHAL library is now built and present in your project as the `$PROJECT/libs/armeabi/libpacktHAL.so` file.

Exploring the GPIO example app

In this section, you will examine the example Android app that performs GPIO interfacing on BBB. The purpose of this application is to demonstrate how to use PacktHAL to perform GPIO read and write processes from within an actual app. PacktHAL provides a set of interfacing functions that you will use to work with GPIOs from within your Android apps. These functions allow you to read the values of input GPIOs and set the values of output GPIOs. The low-level details of the hardware interfacing are implemented in PacktHAL, so you can quickly and easily get your apps interacting with GPIOs.

Before digging through the GPIO app's code, you must install the code to your development system and install the app to your Android system. The source code for the app, as well as a precompiled .apk package, are located in the chapter3.tgz file, which is available for download from the book's website.

Installing the app and source under Windows

Once you have downloaded the chapter3.tgz file, you must decompress and untar it. We will assume that you have copied chapter3.tgz to the root directory of c:\ after downloading it and will decompress it from there. We will refer to your workspace directory as $WORKSPACE.

We will assume that your adb.exe binary is in your current path. If it is not, call adb by using the full path to the adb.exe binary:

1. Open a file explorer window and navigate to the directory.

2. Right-click on the chapter3.tgz file in file explorer and select **Extract Here**.

A directory named c:\gpio now exists, and it contains all of the files for the GPIO example app. You must import this project into your Eclipse ADT workspace:

1. Launch Eclipse ADT.

2. Open the **File** menu and select **Import**.

3. On the **Import** dialog, expand the **Android** folder and highlight **Existing Android Code Into Workspace**. The **Next** button at the bottom of the dialog will become active. Click on it to continue.

4. On the **Import Projects** dialog, type c:\gpio in the **Root Directory** text field. Then, click on the **Refresh** button. The **gpio** project will appear on the list of projects to import.

5. Click on the **Select All** button, then select the checkbox for **Copy projects into workspace**.

6. Click on the **Finish** button to import the gpio app project into your workspace and copy the c:\gpio directory into your $WORKSPACE directory.

All of the project files for the GPIO app are now located in that gpio directory. A prebuilt .apk package for the app is provided in the $WORKSPACE\gpio\bin directory. You can install this .apk package directly to your Android system using adb:

1. Launch cmd.exe for a command prompt window. Using the command prompt, change into the $WORKSPACE\gpio\bin directory:

```
c:\> cd $WORKSPACE\gpio\bin
```

2. Verify that `adb` can see your BBB using the `adb devices` command:

```
c:\$WORKSPACE\gpio\bin> adb devices
List of devices attached
BBBAndroid      device
```

3. Install `gpio.apk` to your Android system via the `install` command in `adb`:

```
c:\$WORKSPACE\gpio\bin> adb install -d gpio.apk
```

4. If you have already installed the `gpio.apk` app once and are now receiving the failure message of `INSTALL_FAILED_ALREADY_EXISTS`, use `adb` to reinstall `gpio.apk`:

```
c:\$WORKSPACE\gpio\bin> adb install -d -r gpio.apk
```

The `gpio.apk` app is now installed on your Android system, and the app's source is now installed in your Eclipse ADT workspace.

Installing the app and source under Linux

Once you have downloaded the `chapter3.tgz` file, you must decompress and untar it. We will assume that you have copied `chapter3.tgz` to your `$HOME` directory after downloading it and will decompress it from there. We will refer to your workspace directory as `$WORKSPACE`.

Use the Linux `tar` command to decompress and untar the `chapter3.tgz` file:

```
$ cd $HOME
$ tar -xvf chapter3.tgz
```

A directory named `gpio` now exists in your `$HOME` directory, and it contains all of the files for the gpio example app. You must import this project into your Eclipse ADT workspace as follows:

1. Launch Eclipse ADT.
2. Open the **File** menu and select **Import**.
3. On the **Import** dialog, expand the `Android` folder and highlight **Existing Android Code Into Workspace**. The **Next** button at the bottom of the dialog will become active. Click on it to continue.
4. On the **Import Projects** dialog, type `$HOME/gpio` (substituting in the full path for `$HOME`) in the **Root Directory** text field. Then, click on the **Refresh** button. The **gpio** project will appear on the list of projects to import.
5. Click on the **Select All** button, then select the checkbox for **Copy projects into workspace**.

6. Click on the **Finish** button to import the gpio app project into your workspace and copy the $HOME/gpio directory into your $WORKSPACE directory.

All of the project files for the app are now located in the $WORKSPACE/gpio directory. A prebuilt .apk package for the gpio project is provided in the gpio/bin directory. You can install this .apk package directly to your Android system using adb:

1. Change into the bin directory of the gpio project:

   ```
   $ cd $WORKSPACE/gpio/bin
   ```

2. Verify that adb can see your BBB using the adb devices command:

   ```
   $ adb devices
   List of devices attached
   BBBAndroid        device
   ```

3. Install gpio.apk to your Android system via the install command in adb:

   ```
   $ adb install -d gpio.apk
   ```

4. If you have already installed the gpio.apk app once and are now receiving the failure message of INSTALL_FAILED_ALREADY_EXISTS, use adb to reinstall gpio.apk:

   ```
   $ adb install -d -r gpio.apk
   ```

The gpio.apk app is now installed on your Android system, and the app's source is now installed in your Eclipse ADT workspace.

The app's user interface

Launch the gpio app on the Android system to see the app's (UI). If you are using a touchscreen cape, you can simply touch the gpio app icon on the screen to launch the app and interact with its UI. If you are using the HDMI for video, connect a USB mouse to the BBB's USB port and use the mouse to click on the gpio app icon to launch the app.

The app uses a very simple UI to interact with the GPIOs. As it is so simple, the only activity that the app has is default MainActivity. The UI consists of only three buttons and text view.

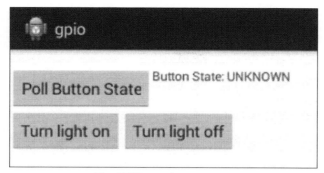

The GPIO sample app screen

The **Poll Button State** button checks the current state of the pushbutton switch and updates the value of the **Button State** text view to report that state. The switch state will be reported as **UNKNOWN** until the **Poll Button State** button is pressed for the first time. The **Turn light on** button will turn on the LED if it is not already on, and the **Turn light off** button will turn the LED off.

The text view has an ID associated with it in `res/layout/activity_main.xml` so that the app can update the text view's value programmatically:

```
<TextView
    ...
    android:text="@string/button_state"
    android:id="@+id/button_state" />
```

Each of the three buttons have an `onClick()` handler defined:

```
<Button
    ...
    android:text="@string/button_poll"
    android:onClick="onClickButtonPollStatus" />
<Button
    ...
    android:text="@string/button_lighton"
    android:onClick="onClickButtonLightOn" />
<Button
    ...
    android:text="@string/button_lightoff"
    android:onClick="onClickButtonLightOff" />
```

Each `onClick()` handler will trigger one of the PacktHAL GPIO functions to read the state of a GPIO or write a new state to a GPIO.

If you need a refresher on the fine details of the various Android UI elements, there are several resources available online that can help you. We recommend that you start with the official Android Developer website at http://developer.android.com/guide/topics/ui/index.html.

Calling the PacktHAL functions

The GPIO interface functionality in PacktHAL is implemented in four C functions:

- openGPIO()
- readGPIO()
- writeGPIO()
- closeGPIO()

The prototypes for these functions are located in the jni/PacktHAL.h header file within the app's project:

```
extern int openGPIO(const int useMmap);
extern int readGPIO(const unsigned int header, const unsigned int
pin);
extern int writeGPIO(const unsigned int header,
    const unsigned int pin, const unsigned int value);
extern void closeGPIO(void);
```

Ideally, you would load the PacktHAL shared library into your app and then simply call the library functions directly to control the GPIOs. The example app actually *does* load the PacktHAL library via a System.loadLibrary() call, but then things become less straightforward because these C functions cannot be called directly. You must specify Java methods that, when called, actually call the C functions.

The MainActivity class specifies four methods with the native keyword to call the PacktHAL C functions in MainActivity.java:

```
public class MainActivity extends Activity {
  private native boolean openGPIO();
private native void closeGPIO();
private native boolean readGPIO(int header, int pin);
private native void writeGPIO(int header, int pin, int val);
```

```
static {
System.loadLibrary("packtHAL");
}
    ...
}
```

These four Java methods specified in `MainActivity` are not actually a direct mapping to the C functions of the same name in PacktHAL. Notice that the GPIO methods in `MainActivity` are all `private native` within the scope of the class. Any method defined with the `native` keyword will attempt to call a native *JNI wrapper function* when it is invoked. However, the naming of the invoked JNI wrapper function follows some very specific rules that represent the scope of its Java-side method. The following figure shows how these JNI wrapper functions finally call the GPIO-interfacing functions inside of PacktHAL:

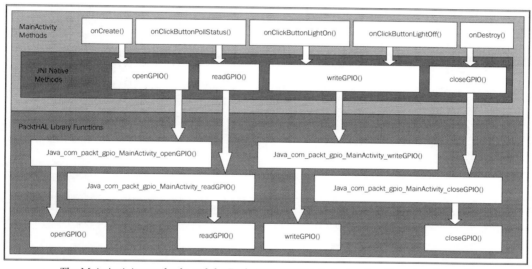

The MainActivity methods and the PacktHAL GPIO-interfacing functions that they call

Each `native` method in the `MainActivity` class with the name `name()` will use JNI to call a JNI wrapper function with the name `Java_com_packt_gpio_MainActivity_name()`. The name of this wrapper function is determined by replacing each `.` in the fully qualified name of the app with an underscore. The `Java_` prefix of the function name tells Android that the function is being called via a method in a Java class. There are a few exceptions to this JNI naming convention, but this general rule will get you through most cases.

Do I need to know all about JNI to make my own Android interfacing projects?

Not really. Using JNI can be quite confusing, and many, many books and tutorials have been dedicated to describing it in great detail. For now, don't worry about not knowing everything that there is to know about JNI. When you have spent some time experimenting with hardware interfacing under Android, you can revisit this topic and learn more of the fine details of how JNI works. In this book, we will focus on showing you just enough information about JNI to get you started.

As an example, our Java openGPIO() method in the MainActivity class for the com.packtpub.gpio example app uses JNI to call the wrapper C function Java_com_packtpub_gpio_MainActivity_openGPIO(). This is a little confusing, but still very manageable. PacktHAL implements these JNI wrapper C functions in the jni/packt_native_gpio.c file. Looking at this source file, you can see where the Java_com_packtpub_gpio_MainActivity_openGPIO() function in PacktHAL calls the openGPIO() C function in PacktHAL:

```
jboolean Java_com_packt_gpio_MainActivity_openGPIO(JNIEnv *env,
  jobject this)
{
  jboolean ret = JNI_TRUE;
  if ( openGPIO(0) == 0 ) {
    __android_log_print(ANDROID_LOG_DEBUG, PACKT_NATIVE_TAG,
        "GPIO Opened.");
  } else {
    __android_log_print(ANDROID_LOG_ERROR, PACKT_NATIVE_TAG,
        "openGPIO() failed!");
    ret = JNI_FALSE;
  }
  return ret;
}
```

Why not just do away with the separate openGPIO() C function and place all of the hardware interface code inside Java_com_packt_gpio_MainActivity_openGPIO()? Functions such as openGPIO() in PacktHAL will usually not change once you have them working properly, and you can use these same functions under both Linux and Android. Wrapper functions such as Java_com_packt_gpio_MainActivity_openGPIO() will change their name and implementation details based upon how and where they are invoked from an app's Java code. It is better to isolate functionality that will not change in its own function. This avoids your accidentally breaking something when customizing or renaming the functions invoked via JNI.

Just remember that a Java method in your app, such as openGPIO() in the MainActivity class, makes a JNI call to invoke a PacktHAL C function with a long, mangled name like Java_com_packt_gpio_ MainActivity_openGPIO(). The JNI wrapper function will then call one of the PacktHAL C functions, for example, openGPIO(), that actually controls the hardware. From the app developer's point of view, once you sort out the JNI wrapper function details, it is almost like calling the C function that controls the hardware directly from the Java app code!

Using the PacktHAL GPIO functions

Now that you have seen how the PacktHAL GPIO functions are called from Java, you will see what each of these functions does and how you can use them.

The openGPIO() function initializes your app's access to GPIOs. This function offers you two different methods for GPIO interfacing, of which you select one method using openGPIO() function's useMmap parameter. The two methods are file I/O (by setting useMmap to 0) and memory-mapping (by setting useMmap to any non-zero number). To change from one interfacing method to the other, you must call closeGPIO() to shut down the GPIO portion of PacktHAL and then call openGPIO() again with a different value for useMmap.

Processes must run as root to use memory- mapping to directly access the GPIO control resistors. As apps cannot run as root, the JNI wrapper function always passes 0 as the useMmap argument to openGPIO() to force the use of file I/O to interact with GPIOs. The openGPIO() method in the MainActivity class does not accept any arguments because of this.

The example app calls the openGPIO() method from the onCreate() method of the MainActivity class:

```
protected void onCreate(Bundle savedInstanceState) {
   ... //Existing statements
   TextView tv = (TextView) findViewById(R.id.button_state);
tv.setText("Button State: UNKNOWN");

   if(openGPIO() == false) {
      Log.e("com.packt", "Unable to open GPIO.");
         finish();
   }
}
```

The complementary call to the `closeGPIO()` method is made by the `onDestroy()` method of the `MainActivity` class:

```
protected void onDestroy() {
    closeGPIO();
}
```

The `readGPIO()` method reads the state of a particular input GPIO. Both the PacktHAL `readGPIO()` function and the `readGPIO()` method in `MainActivity` take the same two parameters. The first parameter is a connector number on the BBB (8 or 9), and the second parameter is a pin location on that connector (1 through 42). The `readGPIO()` method is called from within the `onClick()` handler of the `PollStatus` button:

```
public void onClickPollStatus(View view) {
    String status = readGPIO(9, 13) == true ? "ON" : "OFF";
    TextView tv = (TextView) findViewById(R.id.button_state);
    tv.setText("Button State: " + status);
}
```

In `onClickPollStatus()`, the `readGPIO()` method call is reading the state of the GPIO pin P9.13. This is the GPIO pin that you connected to the pushbutton switch. If the switch is pressed when the `readGPIO()` method is called, `true` is returned. Otherwise, `false` is returned.

The `writeGPIO()` method is used to set the state of an output GPIO. Both the PacktHAL `writeGPIO()` function and the `writeGPIO()` method in `MainActivity` take three parameters. The first parameter is the connector number on the BBB (8 or 9), the second parameter is a pin location on that connector (1 through 42), and the third parameter is the value to set (0 or 1). The `writeGPIO()` method is called from within the `onClick` handlers of the `LightOn` and `LightOff` buttons:

```
public void onClickButtonLightOn(View view) {
    writeGPIO(9, 11, 1);
}

public void onClickButtonLightOff(View view) {
    writeGPIO(9, 11, 0);
}
```

In both of these `onClick()` handlers, the GPIO being set is P9.11. This is the GPIO pin that you connected to the LED. The `onClickButtonLightOn()` method sets the GPIO to 1, turning the LED on. Likewise, the `onClickButtonLightOff()` method sets the GPIO to 0, turning the LED off.

Are you ready for a challenge?

Now that you have seen all of the pieces of the gpio app, why not change it to add new functionality? For a challenge, try changing the app to use only a single button that toggles the state of the LED. If the LED is currently off, pressing the button will turn it on and vice versa. We have provided one possible implementation of this in the `chapter3_challenge.tgz` file, which is available for download from the book's website.

Summary

In this chapter, we introduced you to GPIOs and how they work. You constructed a circuit that uses GPIOs for both input and output, and then you did some basic testing on the circuit to ensure that the circuit was constructed properly and that the kernel is able to interact with the circuit via the filesystem. You also learned about the portions of the PacktHAL `init.{ro.hardware}.rc` file and `BB-PACKTPUB-00A0.dtbo` Device Tree overlay that are responsible for configuring GPIOs and making them available for your app's use.

We showed you how to add PacktHAL into a newly created app project and how to build PacktHAL using the Android NDK. Then, you learned how JNI integrates PacktHAL into your Java app via JNI wrapper functions and explored how each GPIO function of PacktHAL is called and used from within an app.

In the next chapter, you will learn how to integrate I2C bus devices into your apps and begin interacting with hardware that is much more sophisticated than the basic on/off logic of GPIOs.

4

Storing and Retrieving Data with I2C

In the last chapter, you used GPIOs to exchange simple digital data with the outside world. However, what about interfacing with more advanced devices that require complex sequences of bits or bytes for communication?

One of the most popular interfacing buses in use today within embedded systems is the **Inter-Integrated Circuit** serial bus (commonly abbreviated as **IIC**, **I²C**, or **I2C**). In this chapter, you will learn how to write an app that uses the BBB's I2C interface to store data to and retrieve data from a FRAM chip. We will cover the following topics:

- Understanding I2C
- Multiplexing for I2C on the BBB
- Representing I2C devices in the Linux kernel
- Building an I2C interface circuit
- Exploring the I2C FRAM example app

Understanding I2C

Originally developed by Philips Semiconductor in 1982 as a bus for communicating with the ICs, the I2C protocol has become a general-use bus that is supported by a wide variety of IC manufacturers. I2C is a multimaster and multislave bus, though the most common configuration is that of a single master device and one or more slave devices on a single bus. An I2C master device sets the pace for the bus by generating a clock signal, and it initiates communication with the slave devices. Slave devices receive the master's clock signal and respond to the master's queries.

Only four wires are required to communicate via I2C:

- One clock signal (SCL)
- One data signal (SDA)
- A positive supply voltage
- A ground

Requiring only two pins (for the SCL and SDA signals) to communicate with a number of slave devices makes I2C an enticing interfacing option. One of the difficulties in hardware interfacing is effectively allocating a limited number of processor pins to best handle communicating with a large number of different devices simultaneously. By only requiring two processor pins to communicate with a variety of devices, I2C frees up pins that can now be allocated to other tasks.

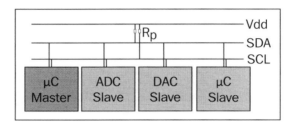

An example of the I2C bus with a single master device and three slave devices

Devices that use I2C

Due to the flexibility and wide usage of the I2C bus, there are many devices that use it for communication. Different varieties of storage devices, such as EEPROM and FRAM ICs, are commonly interfaced via I2C. For example, the EEPROMs present on BBB capes are all accessed by the BBB's processor via I2C. Sensors for temperature, pressure, and humidity, accelerometers, LCD controllers, and stepper motor controllers are all examples of devices that are available through the I2C bus.

Multiplexing for I2C on the BBB

The AM335X processor of the BBB provides three I2C buses:

- I2C0
- I2C1
- I2C2

The BBB exposes the I2C1 and I2C2 buses via its P9 header, but the I2C0 bus is not easily accessible. I2C0 currently provides the communication channel between the BBB's processor and the HDMI framer chip of the built-in HDMI cape, so it should be considered unavailable for your use (unless you would like to void your warranty by soldering wires directly to the traces and chip pins on the BBB).

The I2C1 bus is available for your general use and is often the *go to* bus for I2C interfacing. If I2C1 is at its maximum capacity or unavailable, the I2C2 bus is also available for your use.

Connecting to I2C via the P9 header

By default, I2C1 is not muxed to any pins and I2C2 is available via the P9.19 and P9.20 pins. I2C2 provides I2C communication between the identification EEPROMs present on external cape boards and the kernel's capemgr. You can mux I2C2 to other pins, or even disable it entirely, but if you do so, the capemgr will no longer be able to automatically detect the presence of cape boards that are attached to the BBB. Generally speaking, you probably do not want to do this.

The following figure shows each of the potential pins on the P9 header where I2C signals can be muxed:

I2C1_SCL (Mode2)	17	18	I2C1_SDA (Mode2)
I2C2_SCL (Mode3)	19	20	I2C2_SDA (Mode3)
I2C2_SCL (Mode2)	21	22	I2C2_SDA (Mode2)
	23	24	I2C1_SCL (Mode3)
	25	26	I2C1_SDA (Mode3)

Locations of the I2C buses on the P9 header with different pinmux modes

Multiplexing for I2C

When deciding how you would like your pins to be muxed when using I2C in your projects, keep the following items in mind:

- Avoid muxing any single I2C signal to more than one pin. Doing so wastes one of your pins for no good reason.

- Avoid muxing I2C2 away from its default location, as this prevents the capemgr from automatically detecting cape boards connected to the BBB.

- You can use the default I2C2 bus for your own projects, but note that it is clocked at 100 KHz and the addresses 0x54 through 0x57 are reserved for cape EEPROMs.

- Muxing the I2C1 channel to P9.17 and P9.18 conflicts with the SPI0 channel, so you generally wouldn't want to use this configuration if you also wish to use SPI.

Representing I2C devices in the Linux kernel

I2C buses and devices are exposed in user space as files in the /dev filesystem. I2C buses are exposed as the /dev/i2c-X file, where X is the logical number of the I2C channel. While the hardware signals for the I2C bus are clearly numbered as 0, 1, and 2, the logical channel numbers won't necessarily be the same as their hardware counterparts.

Logical channel numbers are assigned in the order that the I2C channels are initialized in the Device Tree. For example, the I2C2 channel is usually the second I2C channel initialized by the kernel. Therefore, even though it is physical I2C channel 2, it will be logical I2C channel 1 and accessible as the /dev/i2c-1 file.

Underneath all of the layers of Android APIs and services, Android ultimately interacts with device drivers in the kernel by opening files in the /dev and /sys filesystems and then reading, writing, or performing ioctl() calls on those files. While it is possible to interact with any I2C device using only the ioctl() calls on the /dev/i2c-X files to directly control the I2C bus, this approach is complicated and generally should be avoided. Instead, you should try to use a kernel driver that communicates with your device on the I2C bus for you. You can then make ioctl() calls on the file exposed by that kernel driver to easily control your device.

Preparing Android for FRAM use

In *Chapter 2, Interfacing with Android,* you used adb to push two prebuilt files to your Android system. These two files, BB-PACKTPUB-00A0.dtbo and init.{ro. hardware}.rc, configure your Android system to enable a kernel device driver that handles FRAM interfacing, mux the pins to enable the I2C1 bus, and allow your apps to access it.

As far as I2C is concerned, the BB-PACKTPUB-00A0.dtbo overlay muxes the P9.24 and P9.26 pins into the I2C SCL and SDA signals. In the PacktHAL.tgz file, the source code for the overlay is located in the cape/BB-PACKTPUB-00A0.dts file. The code responsible for muxing these two pins is located in the bb_i2c1a1_pins node within fragment@0:

```
/* All I2C1 pins are SLEWCTRL_SLOW, INPUT_PULLUP, MODE3 */
bb_i2c1a1_pins: pinmux_bb_i2c1a1_pins {
    pinctrl-single,pins = <
        0x180 0x73  /* P9.26, i2c1_sda */
        0x184 0x73  /* P9.24, i2c1_scl */
    >;
};
```

While this sets up the muxing, it doesn't assign and configure a device driver to these pins. The fragment@1 node performs this kernel driver allocation:

```
fragment@1 {
    target = <&i2c1>;
    __overlay__ {
        status = "okay";
        pinctrl-names = "default";
        pinctrl-0 = <&bb_i2c1a1_pins>;
        clock-frequency = <400000>;
        #address-cells = <1>;
        #size-cells = <0>;

        /* This is where we specify each I2C device on this bus */
        adafruit_fram: adafruit_fram0@50 {
            /* Kernel driver for this device */
            compatible = "at,24c256";
            /* I2C bus address */
            reg = <0x50>;
        };
    };
};
```

Without going into too much detail, there are four settings in fragment@1 that are of interest to you:

- The first setting is pinctrl-0, which ties this node of the Device Tree to the pins muxed in the bb_i2c1a1_pins node

- The second setting is clock-frequency, which sets the I2C bus speed to 400 KHz

- The third setting is `compatible`, which specifies the particular kernel driver (the `24c256` driver for EEPROM-like devices) that will handle our hardware device
- The last setting is `reg`, which specifies the address on the I2C bus where this device will reside (`0x50`, in our case)

Building an I2C-interfacing circuit

Now that you have an understanding of where I2C devices are connected to the BBB and how the Linux kernel presents an interface to those devices, it is time to connect an I2C device to the BBB.

As we mentioned in *Chapter 1, Introduction to Android and the BeagleBone Black*, you will be interfacing with a FRAM chip in this chapter. Specifically, it is a Fujitsu Semiconductor MB85RC256V FRAM chip. This 8-pin chip provides 32 KB of nonvolatile storage. This particular chip is only available in a **small outline package (SOP)**, which is a surface mount chip that can be difficult to work with when building prototype circuits. Luckily for us, the AdaFruit breakout board for the FRAM already has the chip mounted, which makes prototyping simple and easy.

Don't disassemble your circuit!

The FRAM circuit in this chapter is part of a much larger circuit used in *Chapter 6, Creating a Complete Interfacing Solution*. If you build the circuit as positioned in the diagram (towards the bottom of the breadboard), you can simply leave the FRAM breakout board and wires in place as you build the remaining circuits in this book. This way, it will already be constructed and working when you reach *Chapter 6*.

Connecting the FRAM

Each I2C device must use an address to identify itself on the I2C bus. The FRAM chip that we are using can be configured to use an address in the range of 0x50 to 0x57. This is a common address range for EEPROM devices. The exact address is set by using the address lines (A0, A1, A2) of the breakout board. The FRAM has a base address of 0x50. If the A0, A1, and/or A2 lines are connected to a 3.3 V signal, 0x1, 0x2, and/or 0x4 are added to the address, respectively. For this interfacing project, none of the addressing lines are connected, which results in the FRAM retaining its base address of 0x50 on the I2C bus.

The FRAM breakout board (the A0, A1, and A2 addressing lines are the three right-most terminals of the board)

The addresses of many I2C devices are configurable by connecting the address pins of the device to either the ground or voltage signals. This is because there can be multiple copies of the same device on a single I2C bus. The circuit designer can assign a different address to each device by rewiring the address pins, rather than having to buy different parts with different pre-assigned addresses that do not conflict with each other.

The following figure shows the connections between the FRAM breakout board and the BBB. The four main I2C bus signals (+3.3 V, ground, and I2C SCL/SDA) are made using the pins of the P9 connector, so we've placed the breadboard on the P9 side of the BBB.

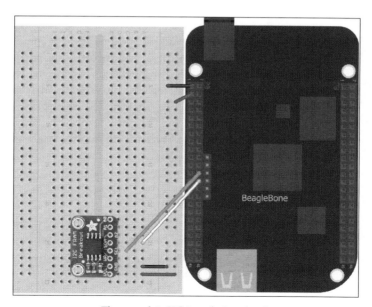

The complete I2C-interfacing circuit

Let's get started:

1.   Connect P9.1 (ground) to the vertical ground bus of the breadboard and connect P9.3 (3.3 V) to the vertical VCC bus of the breadboard. These connections are identical to the ones made for the GPIO breadboard circuit that you created in *Chapter 3, Handling Inputs and Outputs with GPIOs*.

2.   The I2C signals, SCL and SDA, are on the P9.24 and P9.26 pins, respectively. Wire the P9.24 pin to the pin marked SCL on the breakout board, and wire the P9.26 pin to the pin marked SDA on the breakout board.

3.   Wire the ground bus to the GND pin of the breakout board and wire the VCC bus to the VCC pin of the breakout board. Leave the **write protect** (**WP**) pin and the three address pins (A0, A1, A2) unconnected.

The FRAM breakout board is now electrically connected to the BBB and is ready for your use. Double-check your wiring against the diagram of the complete FRAM interfacing circuit to ensure that everything is connected properly.

Checking the FRAM connection with I2C tools

The I2C tools are a set of utilities that allow you to probe and interact with the I2C bus. These tools work on systems that use a Linux kernel, and they are included in the BBBAndroid image. The utilities interact with the I2C bus by opening the /dev/i2c-X device files and making ioctl() calls on them. By default, you must have root access to use i2c-tools, but BBBAndroid reduces the permissions on the /dev/i2c-X files so that any process (including i2c-tools) can read and write information about the I2C buses.

As an example, let's try using the i2cdetect utility in i2c-tools. i2cdetect will sweep a specified I2C bus and identify bus addresses where I2C devices are located. Using the ADB shell, you will probe the i2c-2 physical bus, which is also the second logical bus (/dev/i2c-1):

```
root@beagleboneblack:/ # i2cdetect -y -r 1
     0  1  2  3  4  5  6  7  8  9  a  b  c  d  e  f
00:          -- -- -- -- -- -- -- -- -- -- -- -- --
10: -- -- -- -- -- -- -- -- -- -- -- -- -- -- -- --
20: -- -- -- -- -- -- -- -- -- -- -- -- -- -- -- --
30: -- -- -- -- -- -- -- -- -- -- -- -- -- -- -- --
40: -- -- -- -- -- -- -- -- -- -- -- -- -- -- -- --
50: -- -- -- -- UU UU UU UU -- -- -- -- -- -- -- --
60: -- -- -- -- -- -- -- -- -- -- -- -- -- -- -- --
70: -- -- -- -- -- -- -- --
```

The output of i2cdetect shows every device detected on the current bus. Any address that is not in use has a -- identifier. Any address that is reserved for a device driver in the Device Tree, but does not currently have a device located at that address, has a UU identifier. If a device is detected at a particular address, the device's two-digit hexadecimal address will appear as an identifier in the i2cdetect output.

The output of i2cdetect shows that the Device Tree has allocated drivers for four I2C devices on the i2c-2 physical bus. These four devices are the EEPROMs at addresses 0x54-0x57 of the capemgr. The devices aren't actually present because no cape boards are connected to the BBB, so each address has a UU identifier.

After the FRAM breakout board is electrically connected to the BBB, you must verify that the FRAM is a visible device on the I2C bus. To do this, use i2cdetect to examine the devices present on the i2c-1 physical bus (logical bus 2):

```
root@beagleboneblack:/ # i2cdetect -y -r 2
     0  1  2  3  4  5  6  7  8  9  a  b  c  d  e  f
00:          -- -- -- -- -- -- -- -- -- -- -- --
10: -- -- -- -- -- -- -- -- -- -- -- -- -- -- -- --
20: -- -- -- -- -- -- -- -- -- -- -- -- -- -- -- --
30: -- -- -- -- -- -- -- -- -- -- -- -- -- -- -- --
40: -- -- -- -- -- -- -- -- -- -- -- -- -- -- -- --
50: 50 -- -- -- -- -- -- -- -- -- -- -- -- -- -- --
60: -- -- -- -- -- -- -- -- -- -- -- -- -- -- -- --
70: -- -- -- -- -- -- -- --
```

 Double-check your wiring

If the i2cdetect output shows a UU at the 0x50 address location, you know that the I2C bus does not recognize the FRAM as being attached. Make sure that you don't accidentally swap the SCL (P9.24) and SDA (P9.26) wires when connecting the FRAM breakout board to the BBB.

Exploring the I2C FRAM example app

In this section, we will examine our example Android app that interfaces with the FRAM using I2C on BBB. The purpose of this application is to demonstrate how to use PacktHAL to perform FRAM reads and writes from within an actual app. PacktHAL provides a set of interfacing functions that you will use to work with the FRAM from within your Android apps. These functions allow you to retrieve blocks of data from the FRAM and write new data to be stored on the FRAM. The low-level details of the hardware interfacing are implemented in PacktHAL, so you can quickly and easily get your apps interacting with the FRAM breakout board.

Before digging through the FRAM app's code, you must install the code to your development system and install the app to your Android system. The source code for the app as well as the precompiled `.apk` package, are located in the `chapter4.tgz` file, which is available for download from the Packt website. Follow the same process to download and add the app to your Eclipse ADT environment that was described in *Chapter 3, Handling Inputs and Outputs with GPIOs*.

The app's user interface

Launch the `fram` app on the Android system to see the app's UI. If you are using a touchscreen cape, you can simply touch the **fram** app icon on the screen to launch the app and interact with its UI. If you are using the HDMI for video, connect a USB mouse to the BBB's USB port and use the mouse to click on the **fram** app icon to launch the app. As this app accepts text input from the user, you might find it convenient to connect a USB keyboard to the BBB. Otherwise, you'll be able to use the onscreen Android keyboard to input text.

This app's UI is a bit more complex than that of the GPIO app in the last chapter, but it is still fairly simple. As it is so simple, the only activity that the app has is the default `MainActivity`. The UI consists of two text fields, two buttons, and two text views.

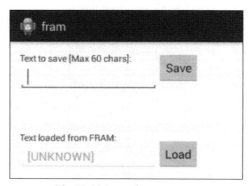

The FRAM sample app screen

The top text field has the `saveEditText` identifier in the `activity_main.xml` file. The `saveEditText` field accepts up to 60 characters that will be stored to the FRAM. The top button with the **Save** label has the `saveButton` identifier. This button has an `onClick()` method called `onClickSaveButton()` that triggers the process of interfacing with the FRAM to store the text contained within the `saveEditText` text field.

The bottom text field has the `loadEditText` identifier. This text field will display any data that is held in the FRAM. The bottom button with the **Load** label has the `loadButton` identifier. This button has an `onClick()` method called `onClickLoadButton()` that triggers the process of interfacing with the FRAM to load the first 60 bytes of data and then updating the text displayed in the `loadEditText` text field.

Calling the PacktHAL FRAM functions

The FRAM interface functionality in PacktHAL is implemented in four C functions:

- `openFRAM()`
- `readFRAM()`
- `writeFRAM()`
- `closeFRAM()`

The prototypes for these functions are located in the `jni/PacktHAL.h` header file within the app's project:

```
extern int openFRAM(const unsigned int bus, const unsigned int
    address);
extern int readFRAM(const unsigned int offset, const unsigned int
    bufferSize, const char *buffer);
extern int writeFRAM(const unsigned int offset, const unsigned int
    const char *buffer);
extern void closeFRAM(void);
```

The `openFRAM()` function opens the file in the `/dev` filesystem that provides the interface to the 24c256 EEPROM kernel driver. Its counterpart function is `closeFRAM()`, which closes this file once hardware interfacing with the FRAM is no longer needed. The `readFRAM()` function reads a buffer of data from the FRAM, and the `writeFRAM()` function writes a buffer of data to the FRAM for persistent storage. Together, these four functions provide all of the necessary functionality that you need to interact with the FRAM.

Just like the `gpio` app from the previous chapter, the `fram` app loads the PacktHAL shared library via a `System.loadLibrary()` call to access the PacktHAL FRAM interface functions and the JNI wrapper functions that call them. However, unlike the `gpio` app, the `MainActivity` class of the `fram` app does not specify methods with the `native` keyword to call the PacktHAL JNI-wrapper C functions. Instead, it leaves the hardware interfacing to an *asynchronous task* class named `HardwareTask`:

```
Public class MainActivity extends Activity {

    Public static HardwareTask hwTask;

    Static {
        System.loadLibrary("packtHAL");
    }
```

Understanding the AsyncTask class

`HardwareTask` extends the `AsyncTask` class, and using it provides a major advantage over the way hardware interfacing is implemented in the `gpio` app. `AsyncTask`s allows you to perform complex and time-consuming hardware-interfacing tasks without your app becoming unresponsive while the tasks are executed. Each instance of an `AsyncTask` class can create a new **thread of execution** within Android. This is similar to how multithreaded programs found on other OSes spin new threads to handle file and network I/O, manage UIs, and perform parallel processing.

In the previous chapter, the `gpio` app only used a single thread during its execution. This thread is the main UI thread that is part of all Android apps. The UI thread is designed to handle UI events as quickly as possible. When you interact with a UI element, that element's handler method is called by the UI thread. For example, clicking a button causes the UI thread to invoke the button's `onClick()` handler. The `onClick()` handler then executes a piece of code and returns to the UI thread.

Android is constantly monitoring the execution of the UI thread. If a handler takes too long to finish its execution, Android shows an **Application Not Responding (ANR)** dialog to the user. You *never* want an ANR dialog to appear to the user. It is a sign that your app is running inefficiently (or even not at all!) by spending too much time in handlers within the UI thread.

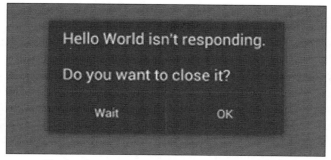

The Application Not Responding dialog in Android

The gpio app in the last chapter performed reads and writes of the GPIO states very quickly from within the UI thread, so the risk of triggering the ANR was very small. Interfacing with the FRAM is a much slower process. With the BBB's I2C bus clocked at its maximum speed of 400 KHz, it takes approximately 25 microseconds to read or write a byte of data when using the FRAM. While this is not a major concern for small writes, reading or writing the entire 32,768 bytes of the FRAM can take close to a full second to execute!

Multiple reads and writes of the full FRAM can easily trigger the ANR dialog, so it is necessary to move these time-consuming activities out of the UI thread. By placing your hardware interfacing into its own AsyncTask class, you decouple the execution of these time-intensive tasks from the execution of the UI thread. This prevents your hardware interfacing from potentially triggering the ANR dialog.

Learning the details of the HardwareTask class

The AsyncTask base class of HardwareTask provides many different methods, which you can further explore by referring to the Android API documentation. The four AsyncTask methods that are of immediate interest for our hardware-interfacing efforts are:

- onPreExecute()
- doInBackground()
- onPostExecute()
- execute()

Of these four methods, only the `doInBackground()` method executes within its own thread. The other three methods all execute within the context of the UI thread. Only the methods that execute within the UI thread context are able to update screen UI elements.

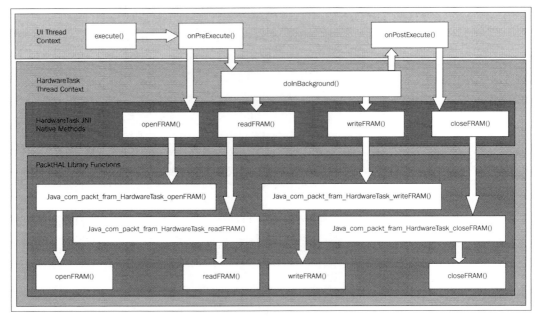

The thread contexts in which the HardwareTask methods and the PacktHAL functions are executed

Much like the `MainActivity` class of the `gpio` app in the last chapter, the `HardwareTask` class provides four `native` methods that are used to call PacktHAL JNI functions related to FRAM hardware interfacing:

```
public class HardwareTask extends AsyncTask<Void, Void, Boolean> {

    private native boolean openFRAM(int bus, int address);
    private native String readFRAM(int offset, int bufferSize);
    private native void writeFRAM(int offset, int bufferSize,
        String buffer);
    private native boolean closeFRAM();
```

The openFRAM() method initializes your app's access to a FRAM located on a logical I2C bus (the bus parameter) and at a particular bus address (the address parameter). Once the connection to a particular FRAM is initialized via an openFRAM() call, all readFRAM() and writeFRAM() calls will be applied to that FRAM until a closeFRAM() call is made.

The readFRAM() method will retrieve a series of bytes from the FRAM and return it as a Java String. A total of bufferSize bytes are retrieved starting at an offset of offset bytes from the start of the FRAM. The writeFRAM() method will store a series of bytes to the FRAM. A total of bufferSize characters from the Java string buffer are stored in the FRAM started at an offset of offset bytes from the start of the FRAM.

In the fram app, the onClick() handlers for the **Load** and **Save** buttons in the MainActivity class each instantiate a new HardwareTask. Immediately after the instantiation of HardwareTask, either the loadFromFRAM() or saveToFRAM() method is called to begin interacting with the FRAM:

```
public void onClickSaveButton(View view) {
    hwTask = new HardwareTask();
    hwTask.saveToFRAM(this);
}

public void onClickLoadButton(View view) {
    hwTask = new HardwareTask();
    hwTask.loadFromFRAM(this);
}
```

Both the loadFromFRAM() and saveToFRAM() methods in the HardwareTask class call the base AsyncTask class execution() method to begin the new thread creation process:

```
public void saveToFRAM(Activity act) {
    mCallerActivity = act;
    isSave = true;
    execute();
}

public void loadFromFRAM(Activity act) {
    mCallerActivity = act;
    isSave = false;
    execute();
}
```

Each `AsyncTask` instance can only have its `execute()` method called once. If you need to run an `AsyncTask` a second time, you must instantiate a new instance of it and call the `execute()` method of the new instance. This is why we instantiate a new instance of `HardwareTask` in the `onClick()` handlers of the **Load** and **Save** buttons, rather than instantiating a single `HardwareTask` instance and then calling its `execute()` method many times.

The `execute()` method automatically calls the `onPreExecute()` method of the `HardwareTask` class. The `onPreExecute()` method performs any initialization that must occur prior to the start of the new thread. In the `fram` app, this requires disabling various UI elements and calling `openFRAM()` to initialize the connection to the FRAM via PacktHAL:

```
protected void onPreExecute() {
    // Some setup goes here
    . . .
    if ( !openFRAM(2, 0x50) ) {
        Log.e("HardwareTask", "Error opening hardware");
        isDone = true;
    }
    // Disable the Buttons and TextFields while talking to the hardware
    saveText.setEnabled(false);
    saveButton.setEnabled(false);
    loadButton.setEnabled(false);
}
```

Disabling your UI elements

When you are performing a background operation, you might wish to keep your app's user from providing more input until the operation is complete. During a FRAM read or write, we do not want the user to press any UI buttons or change the data held within the `saveText` text field. If your UI elements remain enabled all the time, the user can launch multiple `AsyncTask` instances simultaneously by repeatedly hitting the UI buttons. To prevent this, disable any UI elements required to restrict user input until that input is necessary.

Once the `onPreExecute()` method finishes, the `AsyncTask` base class spins a new thread and executes the `doInBackground()` method within that thread. The lifetime of the new thread is only for the duration of the `doInBackground()` method. Once `doInBackground()` returns, the new thread will terminate.

As everything that takes place within the `doInBackground()` method is performed in a background thread, it is the perfect place to perform any time-consuming activities that would trigger an ANR dialog if they were executed from within the UI thread. This means that the slow `readFRAM()` and `writeFRAM()` calls that access the I2C bus and communicate with the FRAM should be made from within `doInBackground()`:

```
protected Boolean doInBackground(Void... params) {
    ...
    Log.i("HardwareTask", "doInBackground: Interfacing with hardware");
    try {
        if (isSave) {
            writeFRAM(0, saveData.length(), saveData);
        } else {
            loadData = readFRAM(0, 61);
        }
    } catch (Exception e) {
        ...
```

The `loadData` and `saveData` string variables used in the `readFRAM()` and `writeFRAM()` calls are both class variables of `HardwareTask`. The `saveData` variable is populated with the contents of the `saveEditText` text field via a `saveEditText.toString()` call in the `HardwareTask` class' `onPreExecute()` method.

How do I update the UI from within an AsyncTask thread?

While the `fram` app does not make use of them in this example, the `AsyncTask` class provides two special methods, `publishProgress()` and `onPublishProgress()`, that are worth mentioning. The `AsyncTask` thread uses these methods to communicate with the UI thread while the `AsyncTask` thread is running. The `publishProgress()` method executes within the `AsyncTask` thread and triggers the execution of `onPublishProgress()` within the UI thread. These methods are commonly used to update progress meters (hence the name `publishProgress`) or other UI elements that cannot be directly updated from within the `AsyncTask` thread. You will use the `publishProgress()` and `onPublishProgress()` methods in *Chapter 6, Creating a Complete Interfacing Solution*.

After `doInBackground()` has completed, the `AsyncTask` thread terminates. This triggers the calling of `doPostExecute()` from the UI thread. The `doPostExecute()` method is used for any post-thread cleanup and updating any UI elements that need to be modified. The `fram` app uses the `closeFRAM()` PacktHAL function to close the current FRAM context that it opened with `openFRAM()` in the `onPreExecute()` method.

```
protected void onPostExecute(Boolean result) {
    if (!closeFRAM()) {
      Log.e("HardwareTask", "Error closing hardware");
    }
    ...
```

The user must now be notified that the task has been completed. If the **Load** button was pressed, then the string displayed in the `loadTextField` widget is updated via the `MainActivity` class `updateLoadedData()` method. If the **Save** button was pressed, a `Toast` message is displayed to notify the user that the save was successful.

```
Log.i("HardwareTask", "onPostExecute: Completed.");
if (isSave) {
    Toast toast = Toast.makeText(mCallerActivity.
getApplicationContext(),
        "Data stored to FRAM", Toast.LENGTH_SHORT);
    toast.show();
} else {
    ((MainActivity)mCallerActivity).updateLoadedData(loadData);
}
```

Giving Toast feedback to the user

The `Toast` class is a great way to provide quick feedback to your app's user. It pops up a small message that disappears after a configurable period of time. If you perform a hardware-related task in the background and you want to notify the user of its completion without changing any UI elements, try using a `Toast` message! `Toast` messages can only be triggered by methods that are executing from within the UI thread.

Unable to access hardware

An example of the `Toast` message

Finally, the onPostExecute() method will re-enable all of the UI elements that were disabled in onPreExecute():

```
saveText.setEnabled(true);
saveButton.setEnabled(true);
loadButton.setEnabled(true);
```

The onPostExecute() method has now finished its execution and the app is back to patiently waiting for the user to make the next fram access request by pressing either the **Load** or **Save** button.

Are you ready for a challenge?

Now that you have seen all of the pieces of the fram app, why not change it to add new functionality? For a challenge, try adding a counter that indicates to the user how many more characters can be entered into the saveText text field before the 60-character limit is reached. We have provided one possible implementation of this in the chapter4_challenge.tgz file, which is available for download from the Packt's website.

Summary

In this chapter, we introduced you to the I2C bus. You constructed a circuit that connected an I2C FRAM breakout board to the BBB, and then you did some basic testing on the circuit using i2cdetect from i2c-tools to ensure that the circuit was constructed properly and the kernel is able to interact with the circuit via the filesystem. You also learned about the portions of the PacktHAL init.{ro. hardware}.rc file and Device Tree overlay that are responsible for configuring and making the I2C bus and I2C device drivers available for your app's use. The fram app in this chapter demonstrated how to use the AsyncTask class to perform time-intensive hardware interfacing tasks without stalling the app's UI thread and triggering the ANR dialog.

In the next chapter, you will learn about the high-speed **serial peripheral interface (SPI)** bus and use it to interface with an environmental sensor.

5

Interfacing with High-speed Sensors Using SPI

In the previous chapter, you worked with the I2C bus to communicate with an FRAM device that requires far more complex communications than that of the simple on/off digital communications used by GPIOs. I2C is very powerful and flexible, but it can be quite slow.

In this chapter, you will learn how to write an Android app that uses the BBB's SPI capabilities to retrieve environmental data from a high-speed sensor. We will cover the following topics:

- Understanding SPI
- Multiplexing for SPI on the BBB
- Representing SPI devices in the Linux kernel
- Building an SPI interface circuit
- Exploring the SPI sensor example app

Understanding SPI

The **Serial Peripheral Interface** (**SPI**) bus is a high-speed, serial bus originally developed by Motorola. Its purpose is to facilitate point-to-point communication between a single master device and one or more slave device. The SPI bus is typically implemented using four signals:

- SCLK
- MOSI
- MISO
- SS/CS

Like I2C, the master on the SPI bus sets the pace of communication between the master and the slave by producing a clock signal. With SPI, this clock signal is called the **serial clock** (SCLK). Unlike the bidirectional data bus of I2C, SPI uses dedicated outgoing and incoming data lines for each device. Using dedicated lines results in SPI being able to achieve communication speeds far higher than those of I2C. The master sends data to the slave via the **master out, slave in** (MOSI) signal, and it receives data from the slave via the **master in, slave out** (MISO) signal. The **slave select** (SS) signal, also called **chip select** (CS), tells the slave device whether it should be awake and paying attention for any clock signals on SCLK and data being sent to it via MOSI. There are variants on this four-wire SPI bus scheme, such as a three-wire scheme that omits the SS/CS signal, but the BBB uses a four-wire scheme for its SPI buses.

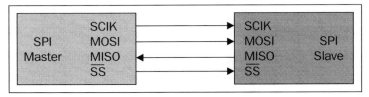

The SPI master and slave devices on an SPI bus

The BBB can act as either an SPI master or slave, so it does not label its data input and output signals for SPI as MISO or MOSI. Instead, it uses the names D0 and D1 for these signals. If the BBB acts as the master on the SPI bus, D0 is the MISO signal and D1 is the MOSI signal. If the BBB acts as the slave on the SPI bus, these are reversed (D1 is MISO, D0 is MOSI). For this book, the BBB will always be acting as the SPI master.

How do I remember which BBB SPI signal is input and which is output?

It can be confusing to remember which signal is MISO and which is MOSI when the BBB uses the signal names D0 and D1. One way to remember is to think of the 0 in D0 as an *O* (for slave output) and the 1 in D1 as an *I* (for slave input). If the BBB is the SPI master (which will almost always be the case), then D1 is the slave input signal (MOSI) and D0 is the slave output signal (MISO).

The maximum SCLK speed for SPI on the BBB is 48 MHz, but speeds ranging from 1 MHz to 16 MHz are commonly used. Even at these reduced clock speeds, SPI is far superior to the 400 KHz clock speed of I2C buses when considering the amount of raw data that can be transmitted each second. Only one device can transmit data on an I2C bus at any time, but both the master and slave can transmit data simultaneously on an SPI bus because each device has a dedicated transmission signal.

Multiplexing for SPI on the BBB

The AM335X processor of the BBB provides two SPI buses: SPI0 and SPI1. Both buses are accessible via the P9 header. By default, no SPI buses are muxed. The following figure shows each of the potential pins on the P9 header where SPI signals can be muxed in different pinmux modes:

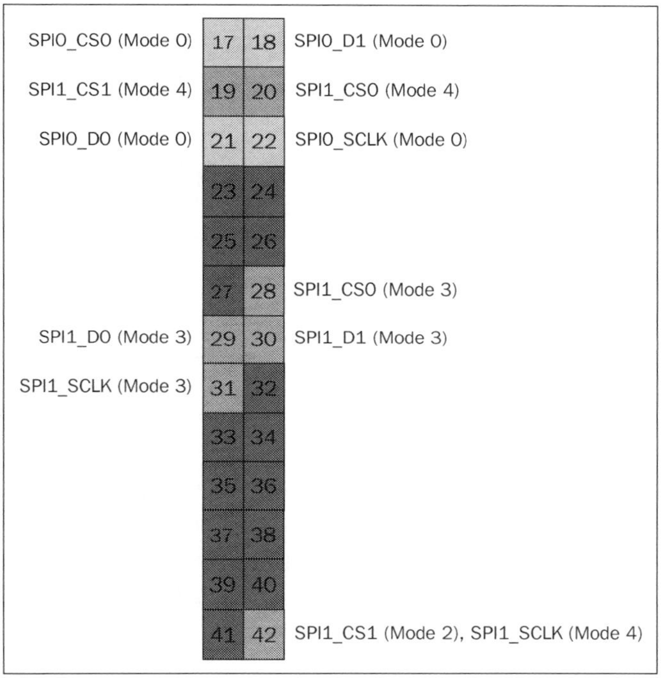

Locations of the SPI buses on the P9 header with different pinmux modes

When deciding how you would like your pins to be muxed using SPI in your projects, keep the following in mind:

- When in doubt, stick with using the SPI0 bus muxed to the P9.17, P9.18, P9.21, and P9.22 pins.

- The SPI1 channel conflicts with the I2C bus used by the capemgr (P9.20) and audio output (P9.28, P9.29, P9.31). Be aware that muxing these pins to use SPI1 can disable some other functionality that you are depending upon for a full-featured Android system.

- If you are using other cape boards in your projects, make sure that these capes don't require the use of the SPI buses. Only one device can exist on each SPI bus unless you use a GPIO pin and extra logic circuitry to manually control each SPI device's chip select signal.

Representing SPI devices in the Linux kernel

The Linux kernel provides a general-purpose SPI driver named spidev. The spidev driver is a simple interface that abstracts many of the housekeeping details involved in SPI communications. The spidev driver is exposed via the /dev filesystem as the /dev/spidevX.Y file. Multiple versions of these spidev files can be present depending upon the number of SPI buses configured in the Device Tree. The X value in the spidev filename refers to the SPI controller number (1 for SPI0 and 2 for SPI1), and the Y value refers to the SPI bus of that controller (0 for the first bus and 1 for the second bus). For the examples in this book, you will only be using the first SPI bus of the SPI0 controller, so /dev/spidev1.0 is the only file with which PacktHAL will interact.

Preparing Android for SPI sensor use

In *Chapter 2, Interfacing with Android*, you used adb to push two prebuilt files to your Android system. These two files, BB-PACKTPUB-00A0.dtbo and init.{ro.hardware}.rc, configure your Android system to enable the spidev kernel device driver that handles SPI bus interfacing, muxes the pins to enable the SPI0 bus, and allow your apps to access them.

As far as SPI is concerned, the BB-PACKTPUB-00A0.dtbo overlay muxes the P9.17, P9.18, P9.21, and P9.22 pins into the SPI CS0, D1, D0, and SCLK signals, respectively. In the PacktHAL.tgz file, the source code for the overlay is located in the cape/BB-PACKTPUB-00A0.dts file. The code responsible for muxing these two pins is located in the bb_spi0_pins node within fragment@0:

```
/* All SPI0 pins are PULL, MODE0 */
bb_spi0_pins: pinmux_bb_spi0_pins {
    pinctrl-single,pins = <
        0x150 0x30  /* P9.22, spi0_sclk, INPUT */
        0x154 0x30  /* P9.21, spi0_do, INPUT */
        0x158 0x10  /* P9.18, spi0_d1, OUTPUT */
        0x15c 0x10  /* P9.17, spi0_cs0, OUTPUT */
    >;
};
```

While this sets up the muxing, it doesn't assign and configure a device driver to these pins. The fragment@2 node performs this kernel driver allocation:

```
fragment@2 {
    target = <&spi0>;
    __overlay__ {
```

```
        #address-cells = <1>;
        #size-cells = <0>;
        status = "okay";
        pinctrl-names = "default";
        pinctrl-0 = <&bb_spi0_pins>;

        channel@0 {
            #address-cells = <1>;
            #size-cells = <0>;
            /* Kernel driver for this device */
            compatible = "spidev";

            reg = <0>;
            /* Setting the max frequency to 16MHz */
            spi-max-frequency = <16000000>;
            spi-cpha;
        };
        ...
    };
};
```

Without digging into the fine details, there are three settings in fragment@2 that are of interest to you:

- pinctrl-0
- compatible
- spi-max-frequency

The first is pinctrl-0, which ties this node of Device Tree to the pins muxed in the bb_spi0_pins node. The second is compatible, which specifies the particular kernel driver, spidev, that will handle our hardware device. The last is spi-max-frequency, which specifies the maximum allowable speed for this SPI bus (16 MHz). 16 MHz is the maximum frequency specified for spidev in the Device Tree overlays provided with the BBB's kernel source.

The custom init.{ro.hardware}.rc file that you pushed to the Android system doesn't have to do anything special for PacktHAL's SPI interfacing. By default, BBBAndroid uses chmod to set the permissions of the /dev/spidev* files to 777 (complete access for everyone). This is not a secure practice since any process on the system can potentially open a spidev device and begin reading and writing to the hardware. For our purposes, though, having the /dev/spidev* files accessible to every process is necessary to allow our unprivileged example app access to the SPI bus.

Building an SPI interface circuit

Now that you have an understanding of where SPI devices are connected to the BBB and how the Linux kernel presents an interface to these devices, it is time to connect an SPI device to the BBB.

As we mentioned in *Chapter 1, Introduction to Android and the BeagleBone Black*, you will be interfacing with a sensor in this chapter. To be specific, we will be using a Bosch Sensortec BMP183 digital pressure sensor. This 7-pin component provides pressure data samples (in 16- to 19-bit resolution) and temperature data samples (in 16-bit resolution) for applications used for navigation, weather forecasting, and to measure changes in vertical elevation and so on.

This particular chip is only available in a **land grid array** (**LGA**), which is a surface mount package that can be difficult to work with when building prototype circuits. Luckily for us, the AdaFruit breakout board for the sensor already has the chip mounted, which makes prototyping simple and easy.

The sensor breakout board (source: www.adafruit.com)

The breakout board labels the SCLK signal as SCK, MOSI as SDI (serial data in), MISO as SDO (serial data out), and SS as CS (chip select). To power the board, a +3.3 V signal is connected to VCC and a ground is connected to GND. The 3Vo signal of the breakout board provides a +3.3 V signal and is not used in our examples.

Don't disassemble your circuit!

The sensor circuit in this chapter is part of a much larger circuit used in *Chapter 6, Creating a Complete Interfacing Solution*. If you build the circuit as it is positioned in the diagram (towards the middle of the breadboard), you can simply leave the sensor breakout board and wires in place as you build the remaining circuits in this book. This way, it will already be constructed and working when you reach *Chapter 6*.

Connecting the sensor

The following figure shows the connections between the sensor breakout board and the BBB. The six main SPI bus signals (+3.3 V, ground, and the SPI SCLK, MISO, MOSI, and SS) are made using the pins of the P9 connector, so we have placed the breadboard on the P9 side of the BBB.

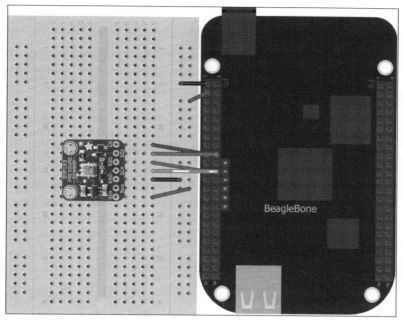

The complete sensor interfacing circuit

Let's get started:

1. Connect P9.1 (ground) to the vertical ground bus of the breadboard and P9.3 (3.3 V) to the vertical VCC bus of the breadboard. These connections are identical to the ones made for the GPIO and I2C breadboard circuits you created in *Chapter 3, Handling Inputs and Outputs with GPIOs* and *Chapter 4, Storing and Retrieving Data with I2C.*

2. The four SPI bus signals, SCLK, MISO (D0), MOSI (D1), and SS are on the P9.22, P9.21, P9.18, and P9.17 pins, respectively. Wire the P9.22 pin to the pin marked SCK on the breakout board, and wire the P9.21 pin to the pin marked SDO. Then, wire the P9.18 pin to the pin marked SDI, and wire P9.17 to the pin marked CS.

3. Wire the ground bus to the GND pin of the breakout board and the VCC bus to the VCC pin of the breakout board. Leave the 3Vo pin of the breakout board unconnected.

The sensor breakout board is now electrically connected to the BBB and is ready for your use. Double-check your wiring against the diagram of the complete sensor interfacing circuit to ensure that everything is connected properly.

Exploring the SPI sensor example app

In this section, you will examine the example Android app that performs the SPI bus interfacing on BBB. The purpose of this application is to demonstrate how to use PacktHAL to perform SPI reads and writes from within an actual app using a set of interfacing functions. These functions allow you to send and receive data between the SPI bus master (the BBB) and the SPI bus slave (the SPI sensor). The low-level details of the hardware interfacing are implemented in PacktHAL, so you can quickly and easily get your apps interacting with the sensor.

Before digging through the SPI app's code, you must install the code to your development system and install the app to your Android system. The source code for the app and the precompiled .apk packages are located in the chapter5.tgz file, which is available for download from Packt's website. Follow the same process to download and add the app to your Eclipse ADT environment that was described in *Chapter 3, Handling Inputs and Outputs with GPIOs* and *Chapter 4, Storing and Retrieving Data with I2C.*

The app's user interface

The app uses a very simple UI to interact with the sensor. As it is so simple, the only activity that the app has (by default) is MainActivity. The UI consists of only one button and two text views.

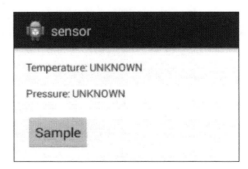

The sensor sample app screen prior to receiving its first set of samples from the sensor

The top text view has the `temperatureTextView` identifier in the `activity_main.xml` file, and the bottom text view has the `pressureTextView` identifier. These text views will display the temperature and pressure data that is retrieved from the sensor. The button with the **Sample** label has the `sampleButton` identifier. This button has an `onClick()` method called `onClickSampleButton()` that triggers the process of interfacing with the sensor to sample the temperature and pressure data and then updating the text displayed in the `temperatureTextView` and `pressureTextView` text views.

Calling the PacktHAL sensor functions

The sensor interface functionality in PacktHAL is implemented in a variety of C functions in the `jni/bmp183.c` file within the `sensor` app's project. These functions not only interface with the sensor, but they also do a variety of conversion and calibration tasks.

The `fram` app in the previous chapter used a specific kernel driver (the `24c256` EEPROM driver) to interact with the FRAM chip, so the user-space-interfacing logic that is implemented in PacktHAL is quite simple. PacktHAL does not use a sensor-specific kernel driver to communicate with the sensor, so it must use the generic `spidev` driver to communicate. It is up to PacktHAL to prepare, send, receive, and interpret the individual bytes of every SPI message that is going to or from the sensor.

While there are a number of functions in PacktHAL to handle these tasks, only four of those functions are used by outside code to interact with the sensor:

- `openSensor()`
- `getSensorTemperature()`
- `getSensorPressure()`
- `closeSensor()`

The prototypes for these functions are located in the `jni/PacktHAL.h` header file:

```
extern int openSensor(void);
extern float getSensorTemperature(void);
extern float getSensorPressure(void);
extern int closeSensor(void);
```

The `openSensor()` function initializes access to the SPI bus by opening `/dev/spidev1.0` and making several `ioctl()` calls to configure the SPI bus' communication parameters (such as the clock rate of `SCLK`).

Once this configuration is performed, all SPI communications performed inside of PacktHAL will use this bus. Calling the counterpart `closeSensor()` function closes the `/dev/spidev1.0` file, which shuts down the SPI bus and frees it for use by other processes on the system. The `getSensorTemperature()` and `getSensorPressure()` functions perform all of the preparation of the SPI messages, SPI communication, and sample conversion logic required to fetch and convert the samples retrieved from the sensor.

> If you were using a specialized kernel driver designed to talk to the specific sensor that we are using, then the sensor-reading logic inside the PacktHAL code would be very simple (only one or two `ioctl()` calls). It is always a balance between placing HAL code logic into the kernel versus keeping it in user space. The more code that you can push into the kernel, the simpler and faster the user space code will be. However, it can be very difficult to develop kernel code, so you must strike a balance between what is easiest to implement and what will provide you with the performance necessary for your hardware design.

The `sensor` app has several similarities to apps from previous chapters. Like the `fram` app from *Chapter 4, Storing and Retrieving Data with I2C*, the sensor app uses its own class derived from `AsyncTask`, `HardwareTask`, to make JNI calls to the underlying sensor-interfacing functions from PacktHAL. Interfacing with the hardware is triggered by the `onClick()` handler of a button pressed by the app's user, similar to what both the `gpio` and `fram` apps do.

Much like the GPIO-interfacing functions from PacktHAL that you used in *Chapter 3, Handling Inputs and Outputs with GPIOs* and *Chapter 4, Storing and Retrieving Data with I2C*, the sensor-interfacing methods in `HardwareTask` are very fast to execute. It is not actually necessary to execute these methods from within a separate thread since they are not likely to take so long to execute that they will trigger the ANR dialog. However, SPI can be used for a wide variety of devices, and it is possible to need longer periods of time to send large amounts of data, so better safe than sorry.

> **When should I use an AsyncTask for hardware interfacing?**
>
> The short answer to this is "all of the time". We did not want to distract you with the details of the `AsyncTask` class when you were working with GPIOs in *Chapter 3, Handling Inputs and Outputs with GPIOs*, so the `gpio` app made method calls to PacktHAL functions in the `onClick()` button handlers. However, the general rule to follow is to always use `AsyncTask` to perform any sort of I/O. I/O is notoriously slow, so any I/O (networking, accessing files on disk, and hardware interfacing) should really take place in its own thread via `AsyncTask`.

Using the HardwareTask class

Like the gpio and fram apps, the HardwareTask class in the sensor app provides four native methods that are used to call the PacktHAL JNI functions related to sensor hardware interfacing:

```
public class HardwareTask extends AsyncTask<Void, Void, Boolean> {

    private native boolean openSensor();
    private native float getSensorTemperature();
    private native float getSensorPressure();
    private native boolean closeSensor();
```

As the details of the SPI bus setup process are encapsulated within the PacktHAL functions and hidden from the app, these methods take no parameters. They simply call their PacktHAL counterparts via the PacktHAL JNI wrapper functions.

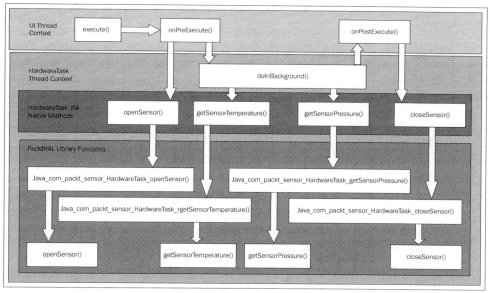

The thread contexts in which the HardwareTask methods and the PacktHAL functions are executed

In the sensor app, the onClick() handler for the sample button in the MainActivity class instantiates a new HardwareTask method. Immediately after this instantiation, the pollSensor() method of HardwareTask is called to request a current set of temperature and pressure data from the sensor:

```
public void onClickSampleButton(View view) {
    hwTask = new HardwareTask();
    hwTask.pollSensor(this);
}
```

The `pollSensor()` method begins the hardware-interfacing process by calling the `execution()` method of the base `AsyncTask` class to create a new thread:

```
public void pollSensor(Activity act) {
  mCallerActivity = act;
  execute();
}
```

The `execute()` method of `AsyncTask` calls the `onPreExecute()` method that the `HardwareTask` uses to initialize the SPI bus via its `openSensor()` native method. The `sampleButton` method is also disabled for the duration of the thread to prevent the possibility of multiple threads trying to use the SPI bus to talk to the sensor simultaneously:

```
protected void onPreExecute() {
    Log.i("HardwareTask", "onPreExecute");
    ...
  if ( !openSensor() ) {
      Log.e("HardwareTask", "Error opening hardware");
    isDone = true;
  }
  // Disable the Button while talking to the hardware
  sampleButton.setEnabled(false);
}
```

Once the `onPreExecute()` method finishes, the `AsyncTask` base class spins a new thread and executes the `doInBackground()` method within that thread. For the sensor app, this is the proper place to perform any SPI bus communication required to get the current temperature and pressure samples from the sensor. The `getSensorTemperature()` and `getSensorPressure()` native methods of the `HardwareTask` class fetch the latest samples from the sensor via the `getSensorTemperature()` and `getSensorPressure()` functions in PacktHAL:

```
protected Boolean doInBackground(Void... params) { ) {

    if (isDone) { // Was the hardware never opened?
      Log.e("HardwareTask", "doInBackground: Skipping hardware
interfacing");
      return true;
    }

    Log.i("HardwareTask", "doInBackground: Interfacing with
hardware");
    try {
```

```
      temperature = getSensorTemperature();
      pressure = getSensorPressure();
    } catch (Exception e) {
      ...
```

After doInBackground() is complete, the AsyncTask thread terminates. This triggers the calling of doPostExecute() from the UI thread. Now, as the app has finished its SPI communication tasks and received the latest temperature and pressure values from the sensor, it is time to close the SPI connection. The doPostExecute() method closes the SPI bus using the closeSensor() native method of the HardwareTask class. The doPostExecute() method then alerts the MainActivity class of the new data received from the sensor via the updateSensorData() method, and it re-enables the **Sample** button of MainActivity:

```
protected void onPostExecute(Boolean result) {
    if (!closeSensor()) {
      Log.e("HardwareTask", "Error closing hardware");
    }
    ...
      Toast toast =
        Toast.makeText(mCallerActivity.getApplicationContext(),
        "Sensor data received", Toast.LENGTH_SHORT);
      toast.show();
      ((MainActivity)mCallerActivity).updateSensorData(temperature,
        pressure);
    ...
    // Reenable the Button after talking to the hardware
    sampleButton.setEnabled(true);
```

The MainActivity class' updateSensorData() method is responsible for updating the displayed values in the temperatureTextView and pressureTextView text views to reflect the newest received sensor values:

```
public void updateSensorData(float temperature, float pressure) {
    Toast toast = Toast.makeText(getApplicationContext(),
        "Displaying new sensor data", Toast.LENGTH_SHORT);
    TextView tv = (TextView) findViewById(R.id.temperatureTextView);
    tv.setText("Temperature: " + temperature);

  tv = (TextView) findViewById(R.id.pressureTextView);
    tv.setText("Pressure: " + pressure);

    toast.show();
}
```

At this point, execution of the `sensor` app has returned to its idle state. If the user clicks on the **Sample** button once more, another `HardwareTask` instance is instantiated and the open-sample-close interaction cycle of the hardware will occur again.

Are you ready for a challenge?

Now that you have seen all of the pieces of the sensor app, why not change it to add some new functionality? For a challenge, try adding a counter that shows how many samples have been taken so far and the average temperature and pressure from all of the samples taken. We have provided one possible implementation of this in the `chapter5_challenge.tgz` file, which is available for download from Packt's website.

Summary

In this chapter, we introduced you to the SPI bus. You constructed a circuit that connected an SPI pressure and temperature sensor breakout board to the BBB, and you learned about the portions of the PacktHAL `init.{ro.hardware}.rc` file's Device Tree overlay that are responsible for configuring and making the SPI bus and `spidev` device driver available for your app's use. The sensor app in this chapter demonstrated how complex tasks in the HAL can be hidden from the app using a small set of functions that hide the low-level details. These simplified PacktHAL function calls can be made from a class derived from `AsyncTask` to perform more complex interfacing tasks simply from within an app.

In the next chapter, you will learn about combining GPIO, I2C, and SPI together into an app capable of providing a complete hardware solution that uses a long-lived hardware-interfacing thread.

6
Creating a Complete Interfacing Solution

In the previous chapters of this book, you interfaced with devices using GPIOs, I2C, and SPI. You used AsyncTasks to perform hardware interfacing in background threads, and you explored how to structure an app to interact with those threads.

In this chapter, you will bring all of these concepts together to create a circuit that uses all three interfacing methods, and you will explore an app that uses all the interfaces together to make a complex system.

In this chapter, we will cover the following topics:

- Building the complete interface circuit
- Exploring the final example app

Building the complete interface circuit

The interfacing circuit used in this chapter is a combination of each of the circuits described in chapters 3, 4, and 5. If you have successfully constructed the circuits from the previous chapters, you already have a good understanding of how the circuit in this chapter will be put together. Leave any previously constructed circuits on the breadboard to save you some effort if you have constructed those circuits by closely following the instructions from earlier chapters.

The following diagram shows the connections between the sensor breakout board, FRAM breakout board, LED, pushbutton switch, resistor, and the BBB. Revisit chapters 3, 4, and 5 for the exact details on how to construct the GPIO, FRAM, and SPI portions of the circuit, if you have not yet done so.

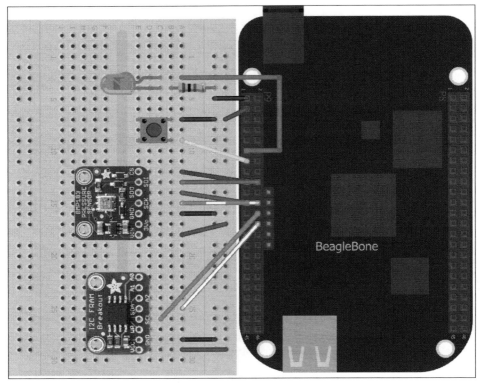

The complete hardware interfacing circuit that uses components which interface with the BBB using the GPIOs, I2C, and SPI components

Exploring the complete example app

In this section, you will examine the example Android app that performs GPIO, I2C, and interfacing on BBB. The purpose of this application is to demonstrate how to use PacktHAL to perform a variety of hardware tasks from within an actual app using a set of interfacing functions. Unlike the previous example apps, which take input from the user, this app takes all of its input directly from the hardware itself. This requires a slightly more complex approach than that taken by the earlier apps.

Before digging through the app's code, you must install the code on your development system and install the app on your Android system. The source code for the app as well as the precompiled `.apk` package is located in the `chapter6.tgz` file, which is available for download from the Packt website. Follow the same process to download and add the app to your Eclipse ADT environment, which was described in *Chapter 3, Handling Inputs and Outputs with GPIOs*.

The app's user interface

Launch the `complete` app on the Android system to see the app's UI. If you are using a touchscreen cape, you can simply touch the `complete` app's icon on the screen to launch the app and interact with its UI. If you are using the HDMI for video, connect a USB mouse to the BBB's USB port and use the mouse to click on the sensor app icon to launch the app.

The app uses a very simple UI that displays two text views in a single activity, which is `MainActivity` by default.

The complete app screen prior to receiving its first set of samples from the sensor

There are no buttons or other UI elements in this app because the only interaction the user has with the app is through the circuit's GPIO pushbutton switch. When the user presses the switch, the app performs a series of hardware interfacing actions:

- The LED will turn on to notify the user that the switch has been recognized as pressed. The LED will remain lit until all events on the list have occurred. While the LED is on, any further switch input is ignored.

- Temperature and pressure samples are fetched from the sensor and written into the FRAM.

- The FRAM is read to retrieve the stored temperature and pressure sample values.

- The values for the temperature and pressure samples are displayed in the app's UI.

- A 1-second delay will occur.

- The LED will turn off, and the switch can once again be pressed to trigger another sample-store-retrieve-display cycle.

The variety of actions performed by the app makes its interfacing behavior more complex than what you saw in the previous example apps in this book. Rather than focusing on interfacing with a single hardware component, this app interfaces with the GPIO, I2C, and SPI devices at the same time to provide a complete sensor solution with persistent storage. However, it is based on the same basic interfacing concepts that the other example apps in this book have demonstrated.

Understanding hardware polling in an app

The earlier apps either used the onClick() handler of a button to interface directly to the hardware (GPIOs) or triggered the instantiation and execution of AsyncTask (I2C and SPI) to interface with the hardware. In both of these cases, interfacing with the hardware is initiated by a software event, the onClick() handler's execution, within the app.

In this chapter's app, however, we want to trigger the hardware interfacing in response to the hardware event created by the switch being pressed. Listening for hardware events is an important part of interfacing because it allows the hardware to tell us when events of interest occur. We do not always have the luxury of telling the hardware to do something and expecting the hardware to do it. Sometimes, the hardware needs to notify us that an event has occurred.

When interfacing with hardware from a kernel driver, the driver can register to be notified of a hardware event of interest by registering for notification of the time a hardware interrupt occurs. A hardware interrupt tells the kernel immediately that something noteworthy has happened with the hardware, and the kernel will stop what it is doing to allow the appropriate kernel driver to handle the interrupt.

Because our apps are performing their higher-level interfacing logic from user space, we are unable to register for an interrupt to notify us the time an event of interest occurs. This hardware event can happen asynchronously at any time, so the app must continually poll, or check, the state of the switch to determine whether it has been pressed or not. Apps typically do not poll for events because they rely on being notified by the Android framework when something interesting happens, but when an app is performing hardware interfacing without the assistance of a manager, polling becomes necessary.

The faster an app polls the hardware, the lesser the chance that the app will miss the occurrence of the hardware event of interest. However, constantly polling in a tight loop is a bad idea because it will constantly consume CPU cycles (and battery life in mobile devices), which can be better spent elsewhere. If you include polling in your apps, you must find a good balance between performance and usage of resources.

It is a bad idea to place a polling loop inside the context of the UI thread. Remember that spending too much time executing within a handler method in the UI thread context will cause Android to trigger the ANR dialog. To avoid this problem, an app must instantiate AsyncTask, which performs the hardware polling in a background thread. The earlier example apps in this book used an AsyncTask thread to perform communication with hardware devices, but the AsyncTask thread was short-lived. The AsyncTask thread's background thread was only active while it was interfacing with the hardware. Once the interfacing was completed, the thread terminated. If the app needed to communicate with the hardware once more, a new AsyncTask thread was instantiated and started via its execute() method.

Because our app must use AsyncTask to continually poll the switch to check for user input, the AsyncTask thread used in the app is a long-lived thread. Instead of instantiating and calling execute() for AsyncTask only at the moments when the app needs to communicate with the hardware, the app instantiates and executes AsyncTask whenever it transitions to the **resumed state**. The AsyncTask thread continues executing in the background until the app transitions to the **paused state**.

 To learn the details of how Android app activities transition among the various lifecycle states, such as the resumed state and paused state, refer to the official Android developer documentation at http://developer.android.com/training/basics/activity-lifecycle/index.html.

Using AsyncTask with long-lived threads

We have already used four methods in the AsyncTask base class in our previous example apps. These methods are used in AsyncTasks to implement both short-lived and long-lived threads:

- onPreExecute()
- doInBackground()
- onPostExecute()
- execute()

In this chapter, you will use five additional methods of the AsyncTask class. These additional methods can be used for short-lived threads to make them more powerful, and they will almost always be used in long-lived background threads to communicate with the thread and receive feedback from it while it runs:

- cancel()
- onCancelled()
- isCancelled()
- publishProgress()
- doPublishProgress()

The cancel(), onCancelled(), and isCancelled() methods are used to stop the currently executing AsyncTask method when the MainActivity class of our app leaves the resumed state. The cancel() method is called from within the UI thread context to notify the AsyncTask class that it has been canceled and should stop its execution. Calling cancel() triggers the calling of the onCancelled() method within the AsyncTask thread context. Then onCancelled() gives the AsyncTask class a chance to perform any necessary cleanup tasks. The isCancelled() method can be called at any time from within the AsyncTask thread context to determine whether cancel() and onCancelled() have been called. This method is usually called from within a loop inside of the doInBackground() method.

The publishProgress() and doPublishProgress() methods allow the AsyncTask thread to notify the UI thread of any information that should be displayed to the user via the app's UI. For example, if an AsyncTask thread is copying a large file from the network, these two methods notify the UI thread how much of the file has been copied and the estimated time remaining to transfer the remainder of the file. The UI thread can then update the UI with this information to keep the app's user informed of the AsyncTask thread's progress.

These five new AsyncTask methods were not used in the example apps in earlier chapters because those apps used AsyncTask methods that were short-lived threads and which updated the screen from the onPostExecute() method. The onPostExecute() method executed within the UI thread, so there was no need to use publishProgress() and doPublishProgress() in those apps. The AsyncTask threads in those apps also executed while the app was in a resumed state, and the threads were so short-lived that it was not necessary to use cancel() or onCancelled() to terminate the threads' execution. Because those apps did not use a loop within their doInBackground() methods, it was not necessary to use isCancelled().

Using the HardwareTask class

Similar to the example apps in previous chapters, the complete app uses a HardwareTask class that is derived from AsyncTask. All of the hardware interfacing is performed via the methods in HardwareTask.

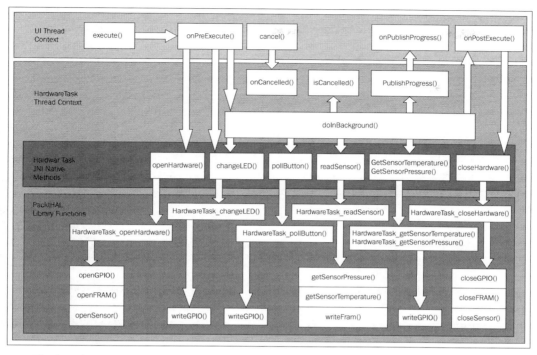

The thread contexts in which the HardwareTask methods and the PacktHAL functions are executed.
The JNI functions in this image have had their function name prefixes shortened to HardwareTask.

The `HardwareTask` class for the sensor app provides seven `native` methods that
are used to call the PacktHAL JNI functions related to GPIO, FRAM, and sensor
hardware interfacing:

```
public class HardwareTask extends AsyncTask<Void, Void, Boolean> {

    private native boolean openHardware();
    private native boolean pollButton();
    private native boolean changeLED(boolean lit);
    private native boolean readSensor();
    private native float getSensorTemperature();
    private native float getSensorPressure();
    private native boolean closeHardware();
```

Because most of the details of the hardware interfacing are encapsulated within
the PacktHAL functions and hidden from the `complete` app, all but one of these
methods accept no parameters at all. They simply call their PacktHAL counterparts
via the PacktHAL JNI wrapper functions. The exception to this is the `changeLED()`
method, which takes a single parameter to specify whether the LED should be
turned on or off.

In the `complete` app, the `onResume()` method of the `MainActivity` class instantiates a new `HardwareTask` class when `MainActivity` changes to the resumed state:

```
public void onResume() {
    super.onResume();

    // Create our background hardware communication thread
    hwTask = new HardwareTask();
    hwTask.pollHardware(this);
}
```

The `pollHardware()` method begins the hardware interfacing process by calling the base `AsyncTask` class `execution()` method to create a new thread:

```
public void pollHardware(Activity act) {
  mCallerActivity = act;
  execute();
}
```

The `onPause()` method of the `MainActivity` class halts the `AsyncTask` class's execution when the `MainActivity` class changes to the paused state:

```
public void onPause() {
    super.onPause();

    // Release the hardware when the app is paused
    if (hwTask != null) {
      hwTask.cancel(true);
      hwTask = null;
    }
}
```

The `cancel()` method of the `AyncTask` base class begins the process of canceling the executing `AsyncTask` thread by calling the `onCancelled()` method in `HardwareTask`. In addition to notifying the `AsyncTask` base class that the execution has been canceled, the `isDone` Boolean flag is set in the `HardwareTask` class:

```
protected void onCancelled() {
    Log.i("HardwareTask", "Cancelled.");
    isDone = true;
}
```

Once `MainActivity` has transitioned to the resumed state, the `pollHardware()` method of `HardwareTask` begins the `AsyncTask` thread's execution. In `onPreExecute()`, the `isDone` flag is reset, and the GPIO, I2C, and SPI devices are all initialized via the `openHardware()` method. If the hardware is successfully initialized, the LED is then turned off via a `changeLED()` call:

```
protected void onPreExecute() {
    Log.i("HardwareTask", "onPreExecute");
    isDone = false;
    ...
    if (!openHardware()) {
      Log.e("HardwareTask", "Error opening hardware");
      isDone = true;
    } else {
      changeLED(false);
    }
}
```

After `onPreExecute()` has completed, the `AsyncTask` background thread begins running. The `doInBackground()` method begins its execution. Because this is a long-lived thread, there is a `while` loop inside `doInBackground()` that will continue to execute until the thread is canceled by the main UI thread:

```
protected Boolean doInBackground(Void... params) {

    ...


    // Poll the button until an error or done
    while (!isDone && !isCancelled()) {
```

The loop begins by polling the state of the pushbutton switch. If the switch is pressed, the hardware interfacing logic will begin communicating with the FRAM and sensor. If the switch is not pressed, then the interfacing logic is skipped. In both cases, a slight delay is added via a `Thread.sleep()` method call to give the background thread an opportunity to sleep and allow other threads to run. This limits the resource consumption of the background thread and gives other processes and threads an opportunity to run:

```
        while (!isDone && !isCancelled()) {
            if (pollButton()) {
...
            }
            Thread.sleep(100);
        }
        ...
        return false;
}
```

If the `pollButton()` method states that the button is pressed, the hardware interfacing logic begins executing. This calls the various native methods that invoke the PacktHAL JNI functions.

First, `changeLED()` turns on the LED to let the user know that a sample is about to be taken:

```
if (!changeLED(true)) {
    Log.e("HardwareTask", "Unable to turn LED on");
}
```

Next, the sensor sample is taken and the result is stored in the FRAM. The `readSensor()` native method interacts with the sensor to retrieve the sample data, and then stores the temperature and pressure samples in the first eight bytes of the memory of the FRAM:

```
if (!readSensor())
{
    Log.e("HardwareTask", "Unable to read sensor");
}
```

 The temperature data is stored as a 4-byte float in the first four bytes of the FRAM, and the pressure data is stored as a 4-byte float in the second four bytes of the FRAM. If you are interested in the details of how this is implemented in the native code, take a look at the `Java_com_packt_complete_HardwareTask_readSensor()` function in the `jni/jni_wrapper.c` file in PacktHAL.

After that, the FRAM is accessed to retrieve the temperature and pressure samples:

```
temperature = getSensorTemperature();
pressure = getSensorPressure();
```

Finally, the main UI thread is updated with the new sample data via the `publishProgress()` method. The thread sleeps for 1 second, and then the LED turns off. At this point, the `pollButton()` check is complete and the `while` loop begins again:

```
publishProgress();
Thread.sleep(1000);
if (!changeLED(false)) {
    Log.e("HardwareTask", "Unable to turn LED off");
}
} // End of pollButton() check
```

The `publishProgress()` method triggers the `onProgressUpdate()` method of `HardwareTask`, which executes in the UI thread. The `onProgressUpdate()` method calls the `MainActivity` class `updateSensorData()` method:

```
protected void onProgressUpdate(Void... values) {
    ((MainActivity)mCallerActivity).
```

```
    updateSensorData(temperature, pressure);
}
```

This `updateSensorData()` method in the `MainActivity` class updates the app's UI and provides a `Toast` message to the user:

```
public void updateSensorData(float temperature, float pressure) {
   Toast toast = Toast.makeText(getApplicationContext(),
      "Updating sensor data", Toast.LENGTH_SHORT);
   TextView tv = (TextView) findViewById(R.id.temperatureTextView);
    tv.setText("Temperature: " + temperature);

  tv = (TextView) findViewById(R.id.pressureTextView);
    tv.setText("Pressure: " + pressure);

    toast.show();
}
```

The main polling `while` loop in the `HardwareTask` class' `doInBackground()` method will eventually exit as a result of either the hardware interfacing failing to initialize or the base `AsyncTask` method being canceled by `MainActivity`. Once the loop has finished, `doInBackground()` will exit and the `AsyncTask` background thread will terminate. The `onPostExecute()` method will then perform any cleanup of items required, such as shutting down the hardware interfacing:

```
protected void onPostExecute(Boolean result) {
  if (!closeHardware()) {
    Log.e("HardwareTask", "Error closing hardware");
  }
    ...
  }
```

The `HardwareTask` instance has now completed its background thread. If the `MainActivity` returns to the resumed state, a new `HardwareTask` instance will be instantiated. This `HardwareTask` instance will create another long-lived background thread, and the hardware interfacing process will repeat itself.

Are you ready for a challenge?

Now that you have seen all of the pieces of the complete app, why not change it to add some new functionality? For a challenge, try changing the app to continually take samples once the button has been pressed. Stop taking samples if the button is held down for a short period of time. We have provided one possible implementation of this in the `chapter6_challenge.tgz` file, which is available for download from the Packt website.

Summary

In this chapter, we introduced the concept of long-lived threads for hardware interfacing. You constructed a circuit that connected the GPIO pushbutton switch, GPIO LED, FRAM device, and temperature and pressure sensors to the BBB. Unlike the example apps in the previous chapters, the example app in this chapter used polling to continually monitor the state of the hardware. You also explored using five additional methods of the `AsyncTask` class for communication and control between the background thread and the main UI thread of your app.

Now that you have learned many of the basic concepts of hardware interfacing with Android using an app, it is time to look at the bigger picture and see how to turn your prototyped solution into a more permanent solution.

In the next chapter, you will learn about integrating your solution with the Android framework, combining your solution with other capes available for the BBB, and other interfaces that you can use for your future interfacing projects.

7
Where to Go from Here

In the previous chapter, we examined how an Android app can interface with GPIO, I2C, and SPI at the same time to provide a complete hardware-interfacing solution. While you might think that this covers most of the problems of hardware interfacing under Android, there are still many other factors to consider.

In this chapter, we will cover the following topics:

- Integrating your solution into Android
- Combining your hardware with other hardware
- Exploring the BBB's other interfaces

Integrating your solution with Android

The BBB offers a wide variety of hardware features, and the particular features that you use in your projects will vary as you change the capes and overlays used within your system. While this gives you a lot of flexibility during prototyping, you might eventually reach a point where you will finalize your custom hardware design to a single, static configuration and decide to make it a permanent Android-based solution.

The examples in this book make the design decision of having apps directly access the hardware of the BBB. While this approach makes creating hardware-interfacing Android apps simple, it is not an ideal approach. Once you have a hardware design that you like and software that properly interfaces with the hardware, it is time to fully integrate your solution with Android. Depending upon just how complex your hardware solution is, you might end up creating custom kernel device drivers, or even modifying the managers within the Android OS framework!

Creating a custom kernel and Device Tree

The first step to creating a permanent Android solution is to ensure that everything on the Linux side of the system is as it should be. This means that all hardware support (such as Linux kernel drivers needed for your project) should be enabled in the kernel and configured and allocated within the kernel's Device Tree (for pin muxing and resource allocation). Ideally, everything that you need will be statically built directly into the kernel and Device Tree. This eliminates the need to load overlays and kernel modules for your solution via explicit commands executed from within the `init.{ro.hardware}.rc` file.

Our advice for preparing the kernel space aspects of your project is to develop these items from within Linux. The Linux environment provides far more tools for kernel driver development and debugging, and you'll be able to quickly and easily build standalone user space binaries that interact with custom and existing kernel drivers via the `open()`, `read()`, `write()`, and `ioctl()` function calls. The code-compile-test-debug cycle of Linux user space binaries can be performed very quickly because a full development toolchain, including compilers and debuggers, are available under Linux. Under Android, you must build such test binaries using the Android NDK on your development machine and then use `adb` to push them to an Android system for test. This makes the development cycle much slower and more difficult.

Developing a static Device Tree for your solution requires a similar process. The Device Tree and its overlays are compiled using the `dtc` tool, which is available under Linux, but not Android. Using standard Linux kernel debugging techniques, you can develop and troubleshoot an overlay that muxes the pins for your project and allocates the necessary kernel drivers to these pins. Once your overlay is working properly, you can integrate the overlay into the Device Tree permanently.

Where can I learn more about Linux development for the BBB?

There are many tutorials and resources available on the web to help you learn about developing Linux software and Device Tree overlays for the BBB. The best resource that we can recommend to you is the series of BeagleBone video tutorials created by Derek Molloy. These tutorials cover topics such as the setup and configuration of a C/C++ development environment, debugging, Device Tree overlay creation, and troubleshooting. They also have a variety of code and circuit examples to help get you started. You can watch these tutorials from the BeagleBone section of Derek's website at `http://derekmolloy.ie/beaglebone`.

Adding hardware communication into the kernel

While interfacing directly with GPIOs and the I2C and SPI buses is convenient, it is not the most efficient way to interface with hardware. The I2C FRAM example in *Chapter 4*, *Storing and Retrieving Data with I2C*, uses the 24c256 kernel driver to handle low-level details of communication with the FRAM chip. Can you imagine how difficult it would be to implement every single detail needed to directly interface with the FRAM chip? Aside from having to know every detail of the communication protocol between the BBB and the FRAM chip, such protocols can also require strict timing guarantees that are difficult or impossible to meet from user space.

In cases where user space interfacing with hardware is infeasible, using a kernel driver is necessary. Kernel drivers encapsulate the details of communicating with a specific piece of hardware. This simplifies your interfacing apps by keeping these details outside your app's implementation. Kernel drivers also provide much stricter timing guarantees when communicating with hardware. This is because the kernel has a much deeper understanding of scheduling kernel driver communication events to meet the necessary deadlines. In user space, a process can be suspended at any time if the kernel's task scheduler has decided to give another process an opportunity to execute. Even if a user space process priority is greatly increased, it will still always have a lower scheduling priority when compared to the priority of kernel-based activities.

Creating a kernel driver can be quite complex, and it is an activity that is far outside the scope of this book. However, if you find yourself trying to meet very tight timing restrictions when communicating with a piece of hardware, you might eventually need to explore the details of kernel device driver development.

Where can I learn more about developing kernel drivers?

The best place to start learning about kernel driver development is the book *Linux Device Drivers* by Corbet, Rubini, and Kroah-Hartman. This book provides comprehensive instructions that walk you through the development process. Even better, the third edition of this book is freely available for download at `http://lwn.net/Kernel/LDD3`. The third edition was originally published in 2005, so it is a bit dated, but the central concepts presented in the book are still valid.

Integrating into existing managers

In *Chapter 5, Interfacing with High-speed Sensors Using SPI*, you interfaced with an SPI-based temperature and pressure sensor. While you communicated with the sensor using the `spidev` kernel driver from a single app, it is far cleaner to have a manager communicate with the sensor instead. This way, all apps can request access to the sensor data by communicating with the manager, rather than having to understand the many details of SPI communications and coordinating access among themselves. It also restricts which apps have permission to interact with the `spidev` driver.

In fact, Android already has a manager, `Android.SensorManager`, that is designed to talk with hardware sensor resources that are commonly found in phones and tablets. Apps communicate with the manager by requesting an instance of the manager and then requesting an object that represents a particular type of sensor:

```
Private final SensorManager mSensorManager;
Private final Sensor mPressure;
Private final Sensor mTemperature;

Public SensorActivity() {
  mSensorManager =
    (SensorManager)getSystemService(SENSOR_SERVICE);
  mPressure =
    mSensorManager.getDefaultSensor(Sensor.TYPE_PRESSURE);
  mTemperature =
    mSensorManager.getDefaultSensor(Sensor.TYPE_TEMPERATURE);
}
```

If `SensorManager` was extended to interface with the SPI sensor that you used in *Chapter 5, Interfacing with High-speed Sensors Using SPI*, your app could have communicated with the sensor via `SensorManager` with only a few lines of Java code! Even better, the file system permissions of the `spidev` device would not have to be set to such an insecure state for apps to communicate with the sensor. Unfortunately, it can be quite difficult to integrate new hardware functionality into an existing manager for a few reasons:

- You must rebuild the appropriate pieces of Android, which typically requires you to build the complete Android source code base at least once. This is a time-consuming (and often quite confusing) process for the inexperienced. The Android Open Source Project provides instructions on how to build Android from source at `https://source.android.com/source`.

- The additional interface logic for your new hardware must be added into the HAL of the manager that you are integrating with. While this is often fairly straightforward, the pieces of the manager's HAL might be scattered throughout the Android code base.

- The new hardware must comply with the framework's API methods that are provided by the manager. Unless you are willing to break API compatibility to add additional attributes and methods to a particular manager's class, you must ensure that your hardware fits the existing interfaces that the manager provides.

While this integration can be difficult, it is often very straightforward. As Android is designed with tablets and phones in mind, any hardware that can potentially be part of a mobile device platform probably already has an Android manager designed to interface with it. `SensorManager` is a good example of this. It is designed to provide sensor information from a variety of different types of sensor hardware. While you will need to integrate some native code into the `SensorManager` HAL to speak with your particular sensor, the communication between the HAL and the `SensorManager` API methods is a fairly simple process.

Where can I find examples of integrating custom hardware into a manager?

Texas Instruments provides a number of **evaluation modules** (**EVMs**) for the various processors that they produce and sell. As many commercial products are based upon these processors, TI freely provides documentation and guidance on how to create custom HAL code that integrates common hardware into Android managers. The best place to begin looking for these details is the documentation of TI's Sitara Android SDK. The SDK's web page is located at http://www.ti.com/tool/androidsdk-sitara.

Creating new managers for custom hardware

If you are integrating a unique piece of hardware into Android, such as the environment sampler you created in *Chapter 6, Creating a Complete Interfacing Solution*, there will probably not be any standard Android manager that provides the necessary API methods for apps to properly communicate with the hardware. In this case, you might consider creating a new type of manager that specifically deals with the unique hardware.

A new manager can be tailored specifically to the hardware that it interacts with. For example, the BBB offers specialized hardware that allows software to communicate with the computers inside most modern vehicles. Such functionality is not available in standard Android mobile devices, so no exists to handle such communication.

Creating a new manager to handle the specific details of using this interface and providing a custom API to use this manager frees apps from having to know the details of such communication. However, this should be considered as a last resort for the following reasons:

- There is no existing manager code to build upon. At best, you might find a simple manager from which to copy the code as a starting point.

- The Android build process must be modified to include building the new manager code. This requires adding the source files for the new manager to the Android makefiles and then verifying that the Android framework is not broken. Building Android is a large and complex task, so making any changes to the process should not be undertaken lightly.

- You must design a proper API to interface with the new manager. As this new interface addition is not part of the standard Android API, apps will be unable to include these API calls unless you specifically add them to your Eclipse ADT installation.

- You must also augment `android.Manifest.permission` to include one or more new permission settings that allow an app to access the functionality of the new manager. As an alternative, you can piggyback on an existing permission or choose to forego using permissions entirely.

Overall, building a custom manager is a lot of work and not for the fainthearted. The process touches many different pieces of the Android framework and requires expertise in the functionality of all of those pieces. If you find yourself in a position where you think you absolutely need to create a new manager to handle your hardware properly via the Android framework, you should consider skipping the manager and using an approach similar to the examples in this book: have your app communicate directly with your hardware using JNI.

Combining your project with other hardware

Now that you have considered how to best modify the software side of your Android system to fully integrate your custom hardware project, let's look at the hardware side of things. Breadboards do a great job of allowing you to rapidly create and change your hardware project designs. Hardware and software co-design is an iterative process, so you might find yourself changing your hardware designs as you develop interfacing software. However, carrying around a breadboard to show off your hardware projects is far from ideal.

Constructing your own prototype capes

Why not create your own custom cape board project? If you have developed the perfect hardware project for your Android system, you should consider making it a stand-alone cape board. Putting your project into a cape form factor makes it easy to integrate it with other cape boards. It also allows you to move your project from place to place without worrying about disturbing the circuit or accidentally disconnecting any breadboard wires.

Creating a professionally laid-out PCB for a custom cape is a very difficult task for the inexperienced. However, you can still construct your own cape board with a little soldering and planning. Adafruit's Proto Cape Kit (product ID 572) is a great place to start. Proto Cape is little more than a generic PCB to hold components that are soldered into semipermanent circuits. If you purchased the BeagleBone Black Starter Pack (product ID 703) that we mentioned in *Chapter 1, Introduction to Android and the BeagleBone Black*, you already have Proto Cape, as it is included in that kit.

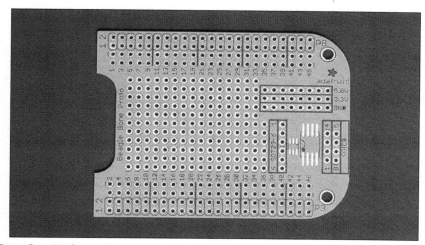

Proto Cape Kit for constructing semipermanent cape circuits (source: www.adafruit.com)

Proto Cape also offers the important advantage of removing the breadboard wires that block the openings of the P8/P9 connectors. Up to four capes can be connected simultaneously by *stacking* the capes (plugging one cape into another via pass-through P8/P9 connectors on each cape). This provides the opportunity to combine different combinations of capes to create a custom Android system that makes the most out of the custom hardware that you have designed. If breadboard wires are blocking the P8/P9 connections, other capes can no longer be inserted into the connectors and stacked on top of the BBB. This makes it impossible to use a breadboard design if the top-most cape in the stack doesn't have a pass-through P8/P9 connector (like most LCD capes).

Commercial capes that interface with Android

There are a number of premade BBB capes that are available for purchase and will work well with Android. 4D Systems (http://www.4dsystems.com.au/) provides several different reasonably priced LCD capes of various sizes and resolutions that are available in both touchscreen and non-touchscreen models. BeagleBoard Toys (http://www.beagleboardtoys.com/) also provides a wide variety of capes, such as LCD, audio, and battery capes. By combining a variety of different capes with your BBB, you can turn your Android system into a portable Android device!

The 4DCAPE-70T (800 x 480 pixels, left) and 4DCAPE-43T (480 x 272 pixels, right)
4D Systems touchscreen LCD capes (source: www.4dsystems.com.au)

What about USB devices?

Other hardware components to consider are USB devices such as audio devices, mice, keyboards, Wi-Fi adapters, Bluetooth adapters, gamepads, and webcams. As the Linux kernel contains drivers for all of these devices, you can easily experiment with them to extend your Android platform and develop a variety of creative apps. The BBB only has a single USB port, though you can connect a USB hub to that port to support using multiple USB devices simultaneously.

Perhaps you can create an Android-based hand-held gaming console with GPIO controller inputs and an SPI- or I2C-based accelerometer. Or you can design a custom automotive control console with a touchscreen LCD that gathers real-time data from your vehicle. You have control of both the hardware and software of the entire platform, and the Android app development tools are excellent for creating UIs quickly and easily. The possibilities are endless!

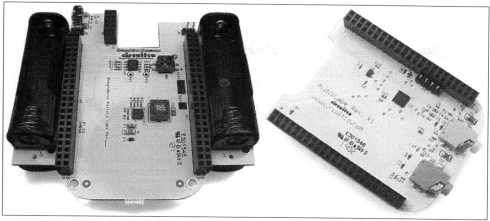

The 5VDC battery (left) and audio CODEC (right) CircuitCo capes
(source: www.beagleboardtoys.com)

Exploring the BBB's other interfaces

So far, we have used the BBB's GPIO, SPI, and I2C functionality for our interfacing. These are not the only interfacing options that the BBB offers, though. The following are a few other interfaces that you should keep in mind as you consider Android projects on the BBB.

Programmable real-time units

Embedded within the BBB's AM335X processor are a pair of programmable real-time units (PRUs). These units are clocked at 200 MHz, so they execute programs at the rate of a single instruction every 5 ns. The kernel loads programs into a PRU and then instructs the PRU to begin execution. Communication between the PRU and the kernel occurs via shared memory. The execution of PRUs is completely separate from that of the main processor, so pushing the PRUs to their limit will not have a performance impact on the main processor unless some coordination between the processor and a PRU is required.

There are a number of GPIO pins that can be muxed so that they fall under the direct control of a PRU. The PRU can check or set the value of these GPIOs on each instruction, meaning that PRU-controlled GPIOs can toggle fast enough to "bit-bang" implementations of complex digital interfaces (such as SPI and I2C). If you have a custom piece of hardware and need to implement a high-speed interface to it, using one or both of the PRUs is an option.

Serial communications

The BBB offers five serial communication UARTs that can be muxed to the pins of the P8 and P9 connectors. There is also a sixth UART (UART0) that provides the serial debug output via the FTDI cable. If you are using the BBB to control a large number of serial-controlled devices, these UARTs are a very useful resource.

Unfortunately, several of these UARTs (UARTs 3, 4, and 5) conflict with pins that are in use by the LCD interface bus that provides video data to LCD capes and the internal HDMI cape. As much of Android's strength comes from its user interface, disabling the LCD interface to receive more UARTs is usually a very poor trade-off. If you find that you absolutely need these UARTs under Android, all of the UARTs can be accessed using the standard Linux kernel serial driver and existing NDK libraries that access the `/dev/TTYS*` files in the filesystem.

Controller area network

There are two **controller area network** (**CAN**) buses on the BBB. CAN is a serial protocol that forms one of the five protocols used in the **on-board diagnostics** (**OBD**) standard for vehicle interfacing. Vehicle diagnostics hardware and software use CAN to communicate with the host controller of most modern automobiles. The CAN driver in the Linux kernel exposes each CAN bus as a network interface that can be communicated with via network socket programming. If you are interested in creating an Android device capable of communicating with your vehicle, such as a status display in your car or a hand-held diagnostic unit, the CAN bus is exactly what you need.

The CAN0 bus is muxed to the P9.19 and P9.20 pins, which are the same pins used by the I2C2 bus used by the capemgr to discover the identity of any connected capes. Muxing the CAN1 bus to the P9.24 and P9.26 pins can conflict with I2C1 depending upon how you have muxed your I2C channels. In general, you won't be able to use SPI, I2C, and CAN at the same time.

The analog-to-digital converter

The BBB isn't limited to only digital communications. It also provides an 8-channel, 12-bit **analog-to-digital converter** (**ADC**) that allows the BBB to receive analog voltage levels between 0 and 1.8 V. This is useful when interacting with real-world sensors as well as many touchscreen displays. However, you must be very careful to ensure that the voltage applied to these pins never exceeds 1.8 volts or you will damage the BBB.

Pins P9.32 through P9.40 are permanently muxed with ADC, so you are free to use them for your own projects. The CircuitCo and 4D Systems LCD capes with touchscreen support presently use ADC channels 4-7 for the touchscreen, leaving channels 0-3 available for your use.

Pulse width modulation

The AM3359 processor on the BBB has a **Pulse Width Modulation (PWM)** subsystem that is used for the precise control of electric motors. PWM sets the period and duty cycle where voltage is supplied to a motor to control its rotation speed. The PWM subsystem contains three **Enhanced High Resolution Pulse Width Modulator (eHRPWM)** modules and an **Enhanced Quadrature Encoder Pulse (eQEP)** module. Altogether, these four modules provide eight PWM channels for driving motors.

While PWM is often seen in control of industrial manufacturing equipment, robotic servo motors, and various other mechanical systems, it can also be used to control the brightness of lighting and other tasks that can make use of the variable duty cycle of PWM to emulate power/brightness/speed levels between off and on at full intensity. If you are interested in controlling mechanical systems with the Android OS, PWM is definitely a feature of the BBB that you should explore further.

Summary

In this chapter, we looked at how to fully integrate your custom hardware projects into Android on the BBB. We discussed how your custom device drivers should be built directly into your Linux kernel and how your custom Device Tree overlays should be compiled directly into the main Device Tree. This avoids having to include a special module and an overlay that loads commands in your `init.{ro.hardware}.rc` file.

We also explored how to customize the standard Android software framework to include support for your custom hardware projects. Existing Android managers can be extended to support custom hardware.

We looked at making your custom hardware design semipermanent using Proto Cape. This allows you to avoid accidentally disconnecting breadboard wires when moving your project around. It also allows for easier integration with commercially available BBB capes by avoiding the problem of blocking the P8/P9 connectors with breadboard wires. We also mentioned that there are many types of USB devices that are also supported by Android and are worth exploring when considering new projects.

Finally, we explored some of the other BBB interfaces that were not covered by the examples in the earlier chapters of this book. The BBB's PRUs, serial UARTs, CAN buses, ADCs, and PWM subsystems all offer additional functionality to interface with the outside world.

Index

Thank you for buying
Android for the BeagleBone Black

About Packt Publishing

Packt, pronounced 'packed', published its first book, *Mastering phpMyAdmin for Effective MySQL Management*, in April 2004, and subsequently continued to specialize in publishing highly focused books on specific technologies and solutions.

Our books and publications share the experiences of your fellow IT professionals in adapting and customizing today's systems, applications, and frameworks. Our solution-based books give you the knowledge and power to customize the software and technologies you're using to get the job done. Packt books are more specific and less general than the IT books you have seen in the past. Our unique business model allows us to bring you more focused information, giving you more of what you need to know, and less of what you don't.

Packt is a modern yet unique publishing company that focuses on producing quality, cutting-edge books for communities of developers, administrators, and newbies alike. For more information, please visit our website at www.packtpub.com.

About Packt Open Source

In 2010, Packt launched two new brands, Packt Open Source and Packt Enterprise, in order to continue its focus on specialization. This book is part of the Packt Open Source brand, home to books published on software built around open source licenses, and offering information to anybody from advanced developers to budding web designers. The Open Source brand also runs Packt's Open Source Royalty Scheme, by which Packt gives a royalty to each open source project about whose software a book is sold.

Writing for Packt

We welcome all inquiries from people who are interested in authoring. Book proposals should be sent to author@packtpub.com. If your book idea is still at an early stage and you would like to discuss it first before writing a formal book proposal, then please contact us; one of our commissioning editors will get in touch with you.

We're not just looking for published authors; if you have strong technical skills but no writing experience, our experienced editors can help you develop a writing career, or simply get some additional reward for your expertise.

BeagleBone for Secret Agents

ISBN: 978-1-78398-604-0   Paperback: 162 pages

Browse anonymously, communicate secretly, and create custom security solutions with the open source software, the BeagleBone Black, and cryptographic hardware

1. Interface with cryptographic hardware to add security to your embedded project, securing you from external threats.

2. Use and build applications with trusted anonymity and security software like Tor and GPG to defend your privacy and confidentiality.

3. Work with low level I/O on BeagleBone Black like I2C, GPIO, and serial interfaces to create custom hardware applications.

BeagleBone Robotic Projects

ISBN: 978-1-78355-932-9   Paperback: 244 pages

Create complex and exciting robotic projects with the BeagleBone Black

1. Get to grips with robotic systems.

2. Communicate with your robot and teach it to detect and respond to its environment.

3. Develop walking, rolling, swimming, and flying robots.

Please check **www.PacktPub.com** for information on our titles

Asynchronous Android

ISBN: 978-1-78328-687-4   Paperback: 146 pages

Harness the power of multi-core mobile processors to build responsive Android applications

1. Learn how to use Android's high-level concurrency constructs to keep your applications smooth and responsive.

2. Leverage the full power of multi-core mobile CPUs to get more work done in less time.

3. From quick calculations to scheduled downloads, each chapter explains the available mechanisms of asynchronous programming in detail.

BeagleBone Home Automation

ISBN: 978-1-78328-573-0   Paperback: 178 pages

Live your sophisticated dream with home automation using BeagleBone

1. Practical approach to home automation using BeagleBone; starting from the very basics of GPIO control and progressing up to building a complete home automation solution.

2. Covers the operating principles of a range of useful environment sensors, including their programming and integration to the server application.

3. Easy-to-follow approach with electronics schematics, wiring diagrams, and controller code all broken down into manageable and easy-to-understand sections.

Please check **www.PacktPub.com** for information on our titles

22629182R00077

Made in the USA
San Bernardino, CA
14 July 2015